Long Challenge:
The Empowerment
Controversy (1967–1977)

by

Victor H. Carpenter

ISBN: 0-9702479-5-8

Editing, design, and layout by Laura Horton
Cover photo by Robert Hoehler

This book is
dedicated to
Henry Hampton

Table of Contents

Introduction vii
By the Rev. William Sinkford

Acknowledgments xi

Chapter 1 1
Beginnings

Chapter 2 23
BURR, BUUC, BAC, FULLBAC, BAWA: The Issue of Leadership

Chapter 3 43
"But Not Both": An Ideology Strained to Its Limits

Illustrations 61

Chapter 4 67
BAC Bonds and the Black Humanist Fellowship

Chapter 5 85
Reflections: The Undiscovered Country

Introduction

I write as the first black president of the Unitarian Universalist Association. With that racial identity and the responsibilities that come with that office, I have not been surprised that Unitarian Universalists expect me to have some simple solution to our lack of racial diversity and our struggles with racism. But solutions here are not simple, despite our wishes.

I lived through the period we call the "Black Empowerment Controversy" as a young Unitarian Universalist. I experienced my own family of origin divided as a result, and the deep sense of betrayal as my faith community "withdrew from commitment to racial justice." How emotionally loaded are the words and labels we use when speaking of that period?

The period itself was emotionally loaded, and like many other Unitarian Universalist people of color I lost my church in its aftermath. Many whites perceived blacks as leaving in anger. The reality is that we left broken-hearted.

And among white UUs, the mistrust, confusion, and betrayal experienced during those years leave many relationships still strained. For 30 years, it has been hard to find trust not only across the racial divides, but around any subject that touches on the issue of race. I have been asked by people on all sides of the "controversy" to find a way to help our faith heal.

"Black Empowerment," "walkout," "racist" . . . the words we use, the language we have to describe the period of the late 1960s and early 1970s are loaded. Why, for example, do we use the term "Black Empowerment Controversy"? It seems to make the anguish of that period the fault of the relatively small group of African American Unitarian

Universalists, rather than the result of the white Unitarian Universalist encounter with race and racism. The term "White Power Controversy" would be more accurate in many ways and would direct attention to the broad Unitarian Universalist movement, and its need for healing and transformation, rather than to the small, marginalized group of "black" people and their allies.

Even now, even for me, it is so easy to get "hooked." So I write with no pretense of objectivity. I will refrain from attempting to tell you the meaning of that time. But I do want to offer a few observations about its residue: That time has not only had ramifications for our address of racism. Silences and the telling of partial truths, which perhaps were inevitable if not intentional, have clogged our spiritual and relational arteries.

Following the Black Empowerment Controversy, Unitarian Universalism went into a period of steep decline. As Victor outlines in this volume, the Controversy was clearly not the only reason, but it perhaps was the most important. Dealing with race, and dealing with conflicts, became threatening. Unitarian Universalism became afraid. The declines in membership and stewardship are easy to document. Harder to document is the spiritual toll the silences and the withdrawal took on our beloved faith. Unitarian Universalist innocence had proven an illusion and our optimism empty of promise—on both sides of the racial divide. After all the engagement and agony of the late 1960s Unitarian Universalism retreated into almost two decades of silence. It was not until the mid-1980s that race was the subject of a GA resolution.

I write with much gratitude to Victor Carpenter. His has been a ministry of healing and truth-telling about this difficult period in our history. *Long Challenge: The Empowerment Controversy* is only the latest chapter. His humility and search for balance show through clearly in his work. Victor has been telling us truth about this period in our history even when we did not want to hear it.

Perhaps enough time has passed for those in my generation to forgive.

Perhaps we are ready: Twenty years of growth in numbers, and years of associational commitment to anti-racism. But most important, perhaps: the complexion of our congregations is changing. The change is not most evident in our pews, though I see some change there as well. The change is in our RE classrooms and youth groups. Transracial adoption, blended families, mixed marriages of many kinds are beginning to make our church schools and youth programs look more like the world.

Perhaps we are ready to ask ourselves what kind of a church we will bequeath to our children—all of our children. We must learn to help our children, all of them, be proud to say, "I am a Unitarian Universalist. This is my church."

The Rev. William Sinkford
President, Unitarian Universalist Association

November 14, 2003

Acknowledgments

This book originated as a series of lectures on the "Black Empowerment Controversy," sponsored by the Minns Lectureship Committee and delivered at the First Unitarian Church of Brooklyn, New York and at Meadville Lombard Theological School in 2002. I wish to thank the Minns Committee for its sponsorship and the First Unitarian Church of Brooklyn and Meadville Lombard for their hospitality. My special thanks to the Rev. Dr. William R. Murry, then-president of Meadville Lombard, for his encouragement leading to the lectures' publication. Thanks to my son Tyler Carpenter, whose computer wizardry helped his father frame the document; to Laura Horton for her editorial skill and insight; and to Cathe Carpenter, whose love and devotion made it all possible.

I am indebted to many people who gave me interviews, comments, suggestions and insights in the course of writing the original lectures which led to this book. They are: the Rev. Wayne B. Arnason, the Rev. Joseph A. Bassett, the Rev. David E. Bumbaugh, Jr., Ronald Cordes, Denny and Jerry Davidoff, the Rev. Clyde Dodder, the Rev. Rose M. Edington, the Rev. William J. Gardner, the Rev. Duke T. Gray, James Gunning, the Rev. John Hickey, the Rev. James A. Hobart, John Hurley, Jackie James, the Rev. William R. Jones, the Rev. Richard Kelloway, Lawrence Ladd, the Rev. Donald W. McKinney, the Rev. Jack Mendelsohn, Samira Mehta, William Norris, Frances E. O'Donnell, Mtangulizi Sanyika (Hayward Henry), the Rev. Carl Scovel, Millie Seaborn, the Rev. William Sinkford, Susan Street, the Rev. Thandeka, the Rev. Lisa Ward, the Rev. Robert West, and the Rev. Farley W. Wheelwright.

Chapter 1

Beginnings

Introduction

The cover story in the May–June 2001 issue of *UU World*, the official journal of the UUA, was devoted to the Unitarian Universalist presence at Selma, Alabama in 1965. The issue's centerpiece is a previously unpublished address by Martin Luther King, Jr., delivered at the memorial service for our Unitarian Universalist martyr James Reeb. In addition to King's remarks, there are reflections by UU clergy who were among the hundred-plus UU ministers present in Selma and an announcement of the dedication of a Reeb Memorial to be located at the Association's national headquarters at 25 Beacon Street in Boston.

Selma marks a turning point in the great civil rights struggle of the 1960s. Reeb and the other UU clergy and laity who journeyed south in answer to King's call for help found themselves on the cutting edge of social change. Following Reeb's martyrdom, they would return home from Selma telling tales of struggle and triumph, pointing with justifiable pride to the UUA banner reading "black and white together," photographed proudly flying over the marchers assembled at the conclusion of the march in front of the Montgomery, Alabama Statehouse.

What is missing from the *UU World* account is any acknowledgement that white Unitarian Universalists in Selma were taking their marching orders not from King directly, but from rank-and-file southern blacks

1

who were occupying positions of civil rights leadership and whose authority was affirmed by whites. Black leadership was apparent at every level of that drama. Had white Unitarian Universalists been more aware of this shift in the traditional ordering of authority, they would have been better equipped to understand what occurred in their own midst only a few months later: the events that have become known as the Black Empowerment Controversy. Their failure to do so is reflected in the clever recent use of a photograph from Selma, in which UUA President Dana Greeley, jaw set in resolute determination, arms locked with those of Jewish and Christian denominational leaders, black as well as white, strides toward confrontation with the Selma police force. In 2000, the *UU World* reprinted the photo four times across the page, each reprint increasingly faded to the point where the people are hardly distinguishable. The story by Warren Ross that accompanies the photo collage is entitled "The UUA Meets Black Power: BAC vs. BAWA, 1967–1971." Ross's article charts the struggle of one denomination to do the right thing but unable to reconcile itself to the ground of racial relations shifting beneath its feet.[1] Judging from this photo collage, showing a strong image of religious commitment gradually fading away, it would appear that in the wake of Selma, the UUs had encountered Black Power and faded away. That was not the case.

The Empowerment story has not received the attention given to Selma. Such telling as has occurred has only succeeded in raising more questions than have been set to rest. For most people in the denomination, many questions remain unclear: Who were the contesting bodies? What separated them from each other? What was the role played by the UUA in the conflict? And why is the controversy labeled "black" when the overwhelming majority of the participants (for we must count all Unitarian Universalists at that time as participants) were "white"?

The Empowerment Controversy spanned a decade (1967–1977) and produced a variety of Unitarian Universalist organizations, each committed to pursuing its particular vision of social justice. These organizations would inspire their members with an intensity of purpose and passion unmatched by any other issue to confront the UUA in its half-century-long history.

Today, some 30 years after the events described here, each participant retains his or her own particular version of events and the meaning of those events. These several meanings have yet to be reconciled and indeed may be irreconcilable. Thirty years later, there is no agreement about the meaning and significance of these events and the place they occupy in Unitarian Universalism's denominational consciousness.

Lacking resolution, the Empowerment Controversy continues to move beneath the surface of Unitarian Universalism's institutional life, generating disquiet. Even its name is in dispute. Names given to particular events have the capacity to obscure or clarify those events, and the name of this controversy is no exception. Calling it the "Black Empowerment Controversy" rather than simply the "Empowerment Controversy" may lead people to assume that the issue was the empowerment of black people by white Unitarian Universalists. The impression is that black Unitarian Universalists were passive recipients rather than vital leaders in the struggle to empower African Americans within the denomination and the larger society.

In addition, the "Black Empowerment" label is a misnomer because it also obscures the fact that whites were empowered in so far as they could enter into active and equal working relationships with African American UUs—mutually empowering relationships that had been previously unavailable because of the conferred social status of "whiteness."[2]

What follows is an interpretive account of the Empowerment Controversy. It is one of several such accounts and makes no claim to be final or definitive. During the period under consideration—from the establishment of a Black Unitarian Universalist Caucus in October 1967 until the final court ruling on Black Affairs Council bonds in 1976—I served as Parish Minister to the First Unitarian Church in Philadelphia and the Arlington Street Church in Boston. I was a member, although not an officer, of both Full Funding for the Black Affairs Council (FULL-BAC) and the Fellowship for Renewal (FFR). In 1983 I published a series of lectures under the title "The Black Empowerment Controversy and the UUA," sponsored by the Minns Committee and subsequently published in tandem with the UUA Commission on Appraisal's report *Empowerment* in 1983.[3]

3

Warren Ross has devoted a portion of his 2001 book *The Premise and the Promise*,[4] a history of the UUA's 40-year existence since the amalgamation of the Unitarian and Universalist denominations into one body in 1961, to the Empowerment Controversy. But neither Ross's brief account of the period nor the Commission on Appraisal's report conveys the wide significance of this moment in our denominational life. It deserves its own book, inviting both a re-examination and a new conversation about the Controversy.

The most important problem in telling this story is that we have no full account or assessment of the conflict by African Americans. The Unitarian Universalist scholar William Jones offers one explanation for this absence: black people, including Unitarian Universalists, had taken hope from the civil rights struggle of the 1960s, perceiving white participation in that struggle as an acknowledgement of the reality of oppression and a willingness on the part of the whites to accept black leadership in addressing that oppression. But subsequent white actions were viewed as a retreat from those insights and a return to deeper denial of systemic racial injustice. As a result African American Unitarian Universalists have had little or no interest in revisiting the Empowerment Controversy or trying to re-engage white UU participation.[5]

The following narrative makes no attempt to rectify that omission. When I first addressed the Controversy 20 years ago in my earlier set of Minns Lectures (1983), I expected that a more complete and inclusive chronicle of events would be written by a member of the Black Unitarian Universalist Caucus (BUUC), the closely related Black Affairs Council (BAC), or the Black Humanist Fellowship (BHF), or perhaps by another African American UU not directly involved in the Controversy's events. No such chronicle has appeared. I believe that my expectations were over-optimistic, derived from an underestimation of the depth of anger and despair in the UU African American community in the wake of what happened.

The lectures from which this book has evolved, originally delivered in 2002, did not deal directly with the events of the Controversy at its height, from October 1967 to June 1969. Therefore, I have included two chapters based on my earlier work on the subject, Chapters 2 and 3, to

4

provide a brief overview of the Controversy and to convey some measure of the excitement and passion that motivated the participants.

In 2001 Unitarian Universalists elected an African American as president of the Association. The Rev. William Sinkford's life has been intimately connected with the contours of the Empowerment Controversy from its beginnings. His relationship to Unitarian Universalism is itself a virtual road map of the progressions and retreats of black Americans who were attracted by the liberal religious vision, became disenchanted by the denomination's failure to live up to and embody that vision, and then returned to embrace the promise that this faith might yet struggle toward fulfillment. The fact of Sinkford's presidency is itself an enormous encouragement to the prospect of an African American version of the Empowerment Controversy story. It is my hope that what follows will serve to encourage a number of members of that community to tell the story that only African Americans can tell and which Unitarian Universalists of all races need to hear and heed.

Acronyms and Acrimony

Selma! One hundred thirty-one Unitarian Universalist white male ministers and double that number of UU female and male laypeople traveled to that Alabama town in March 1965 in response to Dr. Martin Luther King, Jr.'s plea for help in the struggle for voting rights. Three would be martyred. In his moving memoir detailing his 18 days in Selma, the Rev. Richard Leonard has remembered prompting UUA President Dana Greeley to include a mention of the recent murder of a young black man, Jimmy Lee Jackson, in his memorial remarks for the Rev. James Reeb. Greeley thanked him for the reminder of "black and white together."[6]

Because of the strong Unitarian Universalist presence in Selma, the town's name continues to evoke deep personal memories that add to its significance as the turning point in the great civil rights struggle of the 1960s. That one out of every five Unitarian Universalist ministers left their customary church duties in response to King's call, and that the denomination's president and board of trustees would adjourn a scheduled meeting in Boston, fly to Alabama, and re-convene in an African American chapel in this southern town, was astonishing.

These ministers had been called to perform a profound religious witness. It filled them with purpose and hope as well as fear and uncertainty. They were marching with America's greatest civil rights leader of the 20th century in a struggle against an unambiguously evil system of racial hate. Their lives were on the line. For many it was the most thrilling and personally ennobling time in all their years.

Thirty-five years later, the denomination has honored its presence at that moment of historic social change with a bronze memorial at denominational headquarters and the re-publication of King's remarks at Reeb's memorial service. Given the sweeping involvement of UU leaders, such remembrance is appropriate, but, again, absent from much of the re-telling of the Selma story is the role of rank-and-file southern blacks who were occupying position of civil rights leadership and whose authority was affirmed by UU whites.

On the other hand, Leonard's memoir *Call to Selma* shows an outstanding awareness of and acknowledged dependence upon the direction, support, and personal affirmation of African Americans, many of them nameless, many of them children. They companioned him every step of his way.

The companionship of blacks and whites during the civil rights struggles of the early 1960s ended after Selma. After President Lyndon Johnson signed the Voting Rights Act, which restored black citizenship rights under the Fourteenth Amendment, a seismic shift occurred in U.S. race relations. White Americans who had labored for civil rights believed that the struggle had been won with the legislation. They believed that the right to vote was the victory that African Americans had wanted, and that they would be satisfied at having achieved it.

But five days after the Civil Rights Act was signed into law, the Watts section of Los Angeles exploded in a bloody riot that left 35 dead and the white liberal community shaken and confused. The message from Watts that the white community needed to hear was that the right to vote did not necessarily confer power or control over one's community.

Three months after Watts, the phrase "black power" was heard for the first time in public, in a reported conversation between Stokely Carmichael and Floyd McKissick on the James Meredith march through Mississippi in 1966, in which Martin Luther King, Jr. also participated. "Black power" sounded adversarial rather than cooperative. It was not a phrase that Unitarian Universalists were comfortable hearing. For many Unitarian Universalists the ground marked "racial justice" was not only shifting but giving way altogether. A new reality was making itself felt.

The first white Unitarian Universalist leader to acknowledge what was happening and assess its potential impact upon the denomination was the UUA's Director of Social Responsibility, Dr. Homer Jack. Longtime crusader for social justice, Gandhian activist, former director of the National Committee for a Sane Nuclear Policy (SANE), and close associate of Martin Luther King, Jr., Jack was adept at recognizing changes in the social atmosphere and acting accordingly. The Watts riot had been followed by destruction in the inner (black) cities of Newark and Detroit. "Burn, Baby, Burn!" had become an urban slogan. While the smoke was still rising from Newark, Jack urged the UU Commission on Religion and Race to convene an emergency conference called "Unitarian Universalist Response to the Black Rebellion." In his autobiography Jack notes that he chose the title because he felt the situation was something between an urban riot and a full-scale revolution.[7]

During the first seven months of 1967 there were riots in 31 American cities which left 86 persons dead, more than 2,000 injured and over 11,000 arrested. Similar figures could be assembled for the previous three years, leading social observers to speculate that urban rioting was becoming a feature of "mature" capitalism. UU theologian James Luther Adams reflected, "We Americans recognize that ours is the only industrial democracy where one may count upon having riots ever summer."[8]

In September 1967, the UU Department of Social Responsibility published a "Special Report" consisting largely of Dr. Jack's personal observations on the "black rebellion." According to Jack, the disturbances in American cities did not fit the traditional description of "race riot" because blacks and whites were not doing violence to each other; the violence was directed against the society itself, characterized as white. However, the disturbances, chaotic and disorganized as they were, did not indicate the beginnings of a social revolution. The term "rebellion" seemed most appropriate.

In a brief 14 pages, Homer Jack's report presented a portrait of white arrogance and black rage. Yet he saw the rebellion as a sign of "flickering hope that white America may at last be listening. What it hears as shattered must be a new, a revolutionary commitment of our entire society to the Negro and to the cities."[9]

In September 1967, the Rev. Roy Ockert arrived in Los Angeles to serve as Associate Minister at the First Unitarian Church. This was a second career for Ockert, who came to the ministry from a background in organized labor and a life-long interest in the history and theories of working class movements.[10] His experience placed Ockert in a far more advantageous position from which to assess the unrest among African Americans than his fellow white UUs, who were, for the most part, located in suburban, middle-class churches with little or no connection with the experience of blue-collar workers. Ockert's first sermon, "Conflict: Function and Dysfunction," could have been written for the emergency conference in Manhattan: Ockert recognized, as had Martin Luther King, Jr., that racial conflict was necessary if a new awareness of racial power was ever to emerge as a positive force in American life. Ockert was able to translate his experience in labor disputes to the racial struggle, which put him ahead of virtually all the middle-class leaders of the denomination, who generally had little contact with labor, other than from the management side.

Even before he arrived in Los Angeles, Ockert leaned that that a group of African Americans from the First Unitarian Church had gathered together into an organization called BURR (Black Unitarians for Radical Reform), co-chaired by African Americans Louis Gothard and Jules Ramey. It was the first in the dazzling series of acronyms that were to mark both the controversy's progress and eventual demise.

Drawing from his labor experience, Ockert recognized that African Americans suffered from the same problems as workers in the labor market: they needed to withdraw to formulate their own policies and programs even as they participated in integrated organizations. Acknowledging that such tactics of withdrawal could be confusing to whites, Ockert suggested that the white members of First Unitarian form a study group to search for understanding and call the group WURR: White Unitarians for Radical Readjustment.[11]

And so it began. The First Unitarian Society of Los Angeles, a church far removed from UU denominational headquarters both geographically and temperamentally, was the site of the first Unitarian Universalist "black caucus" and the Unitarian Universalist Empowerment Controversy's point of origin. Having received an invitation to attend the Emergency Conference in Manhattan in October 1967, BURR not only accepted but also informed the UUA that it would create a Black Caucus at the Conference and requested that facilities be made available to it for that purpose.[12] Homer Jack granted the request.

On the first evening, 150 delegates and guests gathered at the venerable Biltmore Hotel. The purpose, according to the invitational letter, was "to bring together, by invitation, approximately 125 Unitarian Universalist laymen and ministers to analyze the summer of 1967 riots and to plan how Unitarian Universalists, locally and denominationally, can help to give a new level of commitment to the Black Americans and to the cities by setting new local and denominational priorities."[13] While a wide range of civil rights leaders had been invited to attend and address the Conference, the speakers who accepted reflected the growing edge of the movement towards empowerment. Among them were Floyd McKissick of the Congress of Racial Equality (CORE), a radical secular civil-rights group, and Dr. Nathan Wright Jr. of the Episcopal Diocese of Newark, one of the country's racial hot spots.

The most significant development at the conference was that each of the 37 black delegates was approached by a member of BURR to become part of a black caucus to meet privately, as BURR had requested from Dr. Jack.

The black people who entered the caucus room had little to guide them other than the knowledge that they constituted approximately 1% of the Unitarian Universalist denomination, that their individual records of social and professional achievement separated them from the

American black underclass, and that they identified themselves as black. Their blackness would become absolutely central as the Conference progressed. Blackness was the bonding factor between Caucus members, to the consternation of other black Unitarian Universalists. One of the Caucus members, Judge Wade McCree, who served as the UUA vice-moderator, would ask why these "middle class Negroes whose personal circumstances are so much better in a material sense than the great majority of black Americans, should be concerned about black power."[14] McCree proceeded to answer his own question, testifying that for all black people achieved, the basic acceptance afforded to every white person eluded them simply because of their skin color.[15]

Thus the members of the Black Unitarian Universalist Caucus discovered that their blackness could be a positive binding force of energy and promise. Henry Hampton, then a UUA staff member who would later achieve acclaim as producer of the *Eyes on the Prize* documentary series, reflected on the impact of the Caucus on its membership: "They went into the caucus meeting as middle-class Negroes who had done some individual work in civil rights, but many were far from the struggle and had little to show for it other than their NAACP membership cards. When they came out of the caucus they were still middle-class Negroes, but they were now black, seeking to work through the denomination, giving up the old attempts at harmony and peace for a program of action."[16]

Not all the delegates greeted the formation of the Black Caucus at the outset of the Conference with universal approval. Angry charges of separatism and "reverse racism" were directed at the organizers. Several white delegates attempted to enter the caucus room, only to be turned back by the Rev. Thom Payne, who was stationed as marshal at the door of entry.

Yet the contention over the establishment of a Black Caucus was quickly superseded, first by the Caucus's financial demands and then by the Caucus's demand that its proposals be accepted by the Conference without amendment or debate. The Caucus's report called for black representation on the UUA Board of Trustees, UUA Executive Staff, and the UUA Finance Committee. It called for subsidies for black ministers and for the UUA-affiliated Beacon Press to seek out and to publish black authors. The cornerstone demand, upon which the others rested, was the creation of a UUA-affiliated organization to be known as the Black Affairs Council, to be financed by the UUA with $250,000 a year for a period of four years. The Black Affairs Council was to have sole authority and discrimination over how the money would be spent.

Nothing like this had ever confronted an UUA-sponsored conference before. Suddenly and without warning, white Unitarian Universalism had been challenged. Jeannette Hopkins, a member of the Community Church in New York City, an editor at Harper and Row, and the chair of one of the Conference's commissions, was so offended that she refused to preside for the rest of the session. This, she said, was an appropriate response to the Caucus's "political and racial naïveté, confusion as to goals and priority, dilettantism, and lack of sophistication about the uses of power."[17]

Many, however, had a different response. The black Unitarian Universalists who gathered at the Emergency Conference agreed that the most pressing need was not to protect blacks from white violence, but to empower blacks to challenge white middle-class assumptions. The denomination's traditional patrician mindset of noblesse oblige would not help move it to acknowledge, let alone embrace, a new reality in race relations.

In 1966 Martin Luther King, Jr. had declared that "Negroes have reached the stage of organizational strength and independence to work securely in alliances with whites."[18] The Emergency Conference turned that statement into a question to white Unitarian Universalists. Had white UUs reached the stage of organizational strength and independence to work securely in an alliance with blacks? Much of what occurred during the next several years could be interpreted as a test of that proposition. The events of the Emergency Conference challenged both white and black liberals in a way that was new for a denominational gathering. The radical members of the Caucus told them that their Unitarian Universalist efforts in the cause of liberation were no longer appropriate to the present struggle. The liberals were not immune to criticism for the nation's lack of progress in racial justice. In fact, in some respects, the Caucus argued, liberals were themselves responsible for the failure of adequate understanding and progress. Not only had the liberal demand for racial integration failed to produce justice, it had in effect been a setback for the quality of the lives of black people generally.

Many white and some moderate black Unitarian Universalists greeted this charge with shock, sorrow, consternation, and dismay. "Selma" and the "struggle for integration" were cries still ringing with affirmation in many liberal religious ears. Now they were being asked to accept a plan of denominational action that would be based on racial groups acting separately. This seemed an astonishing reversal of direction that violated their religion's primary principles and purposes.

In retrospect, I believe the most telling critique of integration may be seen not in its failures, but in its successes—for example, when black people are "successfully" integrated into white society. The common assumption was that the black person would abandon those traits which the dominant white society found disagreeable, unacceptable, or offensive. He or she would then, in effect, become "white." Assimilation rather than integration would be the result.

True integration, however, can only occur when people with racial differences come together in an atmosphere of mutual respect for each other's uniqueness, cultural identity, independence, and integrity. Such a vision of true integration is a far cry from the model then being promoted by the majority of white Unitarian Universalists at that time or, in fact, by liberals in general. But this fact did not become generally apparent until several years later when "busing" (the transporting of black schoolchildren into predominantly white classrooms) rocked liberal communities in Boston and other U.S. cities. While the experience might have benefited the white children in the "integrated" classrooms, it had the effect of imposing still further hardships on the black children.

Nor was "busing" the only demonstration of the failure of the liberal model of integration. Unitarian Universalists were involved in many of the struggles for open housing. In practice "open housing" meant allowing a small number of people to escape ghetto living conditions. These people had already achieved a middle-class status and acquired some of the perks of white society. While I applaud their success in breaking down racial housing barriers, it did nothing to change the conditions that continued to entrap the vast majority of the black community in ghetto communities. In addition, often the people who escaped were the people who would have been in the best position to work within the ghetto community for beneficial change. It was the whites who enjoyed the benefits of living with a carefully selected black neighbor.

The majority of the black Unitarian Universalists who attended the Emergency Conference were highly sensitive to the failures of the white model of integration. They recognized that the major beneficiary of integration was the white liberal conscience. The formation of the Black Caucus was a declaration that the liberal integrationist model of social justice was no longer an appropriate expression of their liberal religious values.

The idea of a "caucus" was itself a cause of some consternation for some. The exclusion of white Unitarian Universalists, many of whom were denominational leaders used to being included in the councils of denominational power, was unsettling for both the denominational leaders and those who acknowledged them as leaders. The free religious principle of open covenants, openly arrived at, was being ignored.

The fact is, however, that caucusing had long been a standard way of handling matters of special interest or of concern to particular groups in Unitarian Universalism. At that time, the Humanist Fellowship, the Christian Fellowship, the Woman's Federation and the Laymen's League were all "caucuses," subsets of Unitarian Universalists that met at established times to pursue the concerns of their constituents.

But the Black Caucus was charged with being more isolationist and secretive than any of the other affiliate groups of the denomination. The Black Caucus excluded others from their meetings, whereas other affiliate groups welcomed the seekers and the curious. This was an emotional issue for many of the white Emergency Conference delegates and later, when the Caucus's existence became widely known, for the denominational membership as well.

It was largely a question of identity. Could a black Unitarian Universalist meet with his or her white counterparts as a full and equal partner? Prior to the Emergency Conference the white liberal response was an unqualified "yes." The concept of color blindness was an article of faith for religious liberals. From its enshrined place in King's "dream" speech, it had become a foundational concept for the structure of a progressive moral vision of community. Could a black person come as an equal, come as a full person, come with confidence into this denomination and into its meetings? The whites had always assumed the answer was yes, that color was inconsequential.

But color *is* consequential. Again and again the black delegates said that they could not participate as equals, as full people, with confidence—that skin color was not only important, but decisive, even if only in the subtle ways that whites had not understood.

At the Emergency Conference, the Unitarian Universalist community divided into those who accepted and those who could not accept this explanation of racial difference and its importance.

The black Unitarian Universalists at the Emergency Conference revealed painful truths to the white delegates: The history of black people in America was the history of racial difference and how it had shaped the personhood of blacks and whites alike. Social discrimination and contempt had produced in blacks a lack of self-worth. It had fostered in blacks an acceptance of the inferiority whites ascribed to them, which, in turn, had fostered an attitude of superiority in whites. The ultimate expression of white superiority was the disappearance of "white" as a racial category altogether, becoming the unspoken norm of society to which other races might aspire. The message of the black delegates was that if the U.S. social system in general and the dynamics of Unitarian Universalism in particular, which were inherently oppressive to black people, were to be broken, blacks must achieve a sense of their own dignity, free from any control by whites.

The blacks attending the Conference felt the need to establish this beachhead of freedom for themselves during the proceedings. But they also built into their resolutions their need for the UUA to recognize their liberation efforts by organizing a Black Affairs Council and other special efforts to promote black consciousness.

This was no repudiation of the denomination. It was, in fact, an affirmation of trust that an overwhelmingly white organization would be able to break out of its "whiteness." Nowhere in the Conference documents is there a suggestion of going outside the denomination to bring about the desired changes.

Yet it was a lot for many of the white delegates, and some of the black delegates, to understand or accept. Even for those who had spent much of their lives in the struggle for racial equality, the situation at the Conference proved highly unsettling. The greatest point of controversy occurred when the chairman of the Black Caucus demanded that the Conference give unqualified and total endorsement to the Caucus's proposals without any discussion or revision.

Even those delegates who felt that the Caucus report was reasonable were disturbed by such a demand. It sounded totalitarian and foreign to the democratic traditions of Unitarian Universalism. Many understood it as a demand to renounce a fundamental principle. One explanation offered by the Black Caucus leadership was that whites had long discussed what needed to be done to empower blacks, and there had been no resolution of racial problems. That being the case, whites should be willing to let blacks set their own agenda and call the terms of action. This was not an argument geared to win over whites who were not themselves already convinced that Unitarian Universalism needed black leadership.

White Conference delegates recognized that they faced a conflict between two long-held values: using the democratic process of group discussion and affirming the leadership of minority groups in the struggle for racial justice. Faced with an agonizing decision, a substantial majority of the white delegates voted in favor of the Black Caucus resolution and black self-determination. Their decision would be argued and re-argued for years afterward with the benefit of hindsight. At the time of the decision, limited time constrained the delegates' choices and options. But the decision would have profound consequences, shaping the history of Unitarian Universalism for the remaining decades of the 20th century.

A Personal Note

I did not travel to Selma, Alabama to march with Dr. King in 1965, nor did I attend the Emergency Conference that witnessed the birth of the Unitarian Universalist Black Caucus in 1967. From 1962 through 1967 I was serving as minister of the Unitarian Church in Cape Town, South Africa.

During my years in South Africa, no significant political black organization was permitted to exist. The only organizations that gained government approval were those directly controlled by or fully in agreement with the government's policy of radical separation of the races. South Africa was a textbook example of a fascist state, a totalitarian government that emphasized extreme nationalist principles and incorporated racism as fundamental to its constitutional structure.

One could, and many did, speak out against this sanctioned and codified violation of human rights. Having engaged in this practice, however, I came to realize that individual denunciations of government policies were ineffective. Such speech was, in fact, counterproductive in that it served the government as a pressure vent. It was only when speech led to organization that the government would act.

I had been a member of one organization that attempted to supply legal defense for persons charged with political crimes. After some success, the organization itself was branded a "communist front," its members "banned" (prohibited from attending meetings or gatherings, speaking publicly, or publishing anything) or, worse, subjected to house arrest. Shortly thereafter I returned to the United States, for several reasons. I was under observation by the Special Branch of the South African police force, the branch concerned with political crimes. Since I was an American citizen, my arrest would only have resulted in my being declared "persona non grata" and deported, but any political effectiveness I might have had was at an end. My ministry to the Cape Town church was in danger of being compromised. Finally, our two daughters were both in need of medical attention that was unavailable in South Africa. I arrived home two months after the New York conference at which BUUC was born, and at the beginning of 1968 I began my ministry to the First Church in Philadelphia, PA.

Within a month of my arrival I met with my colleagues the Rev. David Parke and the Rev. Rudolph Gelsey. Each was serving a UU church in Philadelphia, each had attended the Emergency Conference, each recognized the historic dimension of what had happened. Both would emerge as leaders of a white group soon to be gathered to support a bold black UU initiative, the Black Unitarian Universalist Caucus. They were excited by what was taking place within Unitarian Universalism.

Inspired by the Emergency Conference, Gelsey and Parke described for me the Conference's vision of an organization in which black Unitarian Universalists could discover each other and honor the beauty of their blackness as expressed in history, culture, and lifestyle. The Black UU Caucus would be an instrument to build cooperative, program-oriented relationships with other black-oriented organizations in the U.S. and to address public issues affecting black people. Its very presence would sensitize whites to the need for unity, power, and self-determination among black people.

Unlike many of my UU ministerial colleagues who were confused by what had happened at the Biltmore Conference, the news of the first assembly of what would become the BUUC was thrilling to me. Here in my country, black members of my own denomination were demanding the right to organize themselves and to control and direct their struggle for freedom within Unitarian Universalism, without the participation or the direction of white UUs. I was fresh from apartheid South Africa, where such proposals were not only unthinkable dreams, but illegal and punishable offenses. During the time of my ministry in Cape Town, any gathering of black people for purposes other than those sanctioned by whites was a dangerous and potentially imprisonable action. One year after my arrival in South Africa, Nelson Mandela had narrowly escaped being executed and had begun to serve a 27-year imprisonment on Robbin Island for his attempts to organize the South African freedom struggle. After five years in apartheid-land, what I was hearing from my two colleagues was all but unimaginable: black men and women asserting their right to define and lead their struggle for liberation. It was a dream beyond anything that I could have envisioned while in South Africa in the 1960s. And here it was being described to me as actually occurring in my own Unitarian Universalist denomination. I was stunned by the vision of the Black UU Caucus and thrilled by the prospect of the vision's implementation.

My enthusiasm for the Caucus was an echo of what some Conference participants have since called a life-transforming experience. Henry Hampton, then the only African American professionally employed as a member of UUA Headquarters staff, has written, "to have been black and a member of the Black Caucus was to undergo a basic and passionate change; for the first time I was at one with my fellow liberals."[19]

Others had a very different reaction. UUA staffer Robert E. Jones has argued that "the Black Caucus, with its accompanying secrecy and discipline, distrust and inhospitality, was completely unnecessary in the context of a Unitarian Universalist gathering. Assembled in N.Y. were whites and Negroes who shared a common religious allegiance and had long been workers in the civil rights demonstrations; some had even been in jail for the cause; and yet they were to be humiliated—in effect, kicked in the face by their black brothers."[20]

The Rev. Jack Mendelsohn, then-minister of the Arlington Street Church in Boston, who was as close as any white person to the beating heart of the Emergency Conference and the creation of the Black Caucus, reported to his congregation on the events with a prescience that would be born out by later events: "Had the Black Caucus not convened, created its mystique and traumatized the rest of us, we would inevitably have composed a bravely militant set of proposals which would have changed not one iota our familiar denominational racial routines."[21]

It fell to Samuel Beecher, an attorney and UUA board member, to write the most perceptive and, indeed, prophetic comment on the Conference's proceedings. Three days after the Conference, in a letter to Joseph Fisher, the UUA Moderator, Beecher wrote:

> I do feel, however, that we are faced with a new situation in the Civil Rights Movement which is different than that with which we have had to deal, or, had the opportunity to deal with, in the past. For my own part, although some of the proposals show the usual lack of understanding of the financial position of the Denomination, I have come to believe that their desire for "self-determination" is a valid one and deserves serious consideration by our Denomination. One last comment, and that is that this is a situation which will not improve by temporizing and trying to put off to a later meeting of the Board. This is a matter which needs to be dealt with promptly in order

that it may be handled creatively long before the May meeting of the General Assembly which, I believe, if it came up for the first time it would cause very serious division within the Denomination because of the lack of understanding on the part of persons of good will on both sides.[22]

The letter was a tip-off to what was coming. In light of it, UUA President Dana Greeley wrote to Fisher and the members of the Board of Trustees arguing that the UUA November 1967 Board Meeting should be extended for an extra day in order to receive a delegation from the Black Caucus. Having received reports from the Emergency Conference, Greeley wrote:

> This was a very intense and controversial conference, but the Conference endorsed the rather extreme requests of the Black Caucus; and we believe it both right and prudent to give the Caucus a hearing. The members wish to be assisted in organizing a Black Power organization or a "Black Affairs Council" within the denomination. This will not be a perfunctory or easy discussion.[23]

The November 1967 UUA board meeting lived up to Greeley's expectations. The board was divided from the outset. It refused to follow the Emergency Conference's example of complete acceptance or rejection of the Black Caucus's proposals. It reaffirmed its insistence on an integrated society. It willed that the established denominational Commission on Race and Religion be reorganized to include more black persons, with an invitation to the members of the BUUC to participate. BUUC members left the meeting feeling insulted and betrayed. By ignoring the warning in Beecher's letter, the UUA Board had fulfilled Mendelsohn's prediction about "familiar denominational racial routines." The Empowerment Controversy had begun.

Notes

1. Warren Ross, "The UUA Meets Black Power: BAC vs. BAWA, 1967–1971," *UU World* March/April 2000. The article title is misleading in that it suggests that "BAC vs. BAWA" was the locus of the struggle, rather than BAC (and FULLBAC) vs. the UUA.
2. Michael Eric Dyson, scholar and author of *Race Rules: Navigating the Color Line* (Cambridge: MA, Perseus Publishing, 1996) identifies whiteness as a sociological construct involving identity, ideology and institutionality. In a recent interview he says that, as such, it is "the most powerful, sustaining myth of American culture since its inception" (Ronald E. Chennault, "Giving Whiteness a Black Eye: An Interview with Michael Eric Dyson," in Joe Kincheloe et al., eds., *White Reign: Deploying Whiteness in America*, New York: St. Martin's Griffin Press, 1998, p. 301). During the 1990s whiteness was addressed by a host of scholars, including Unitarian Universalist Thandeka, whose book *Learning to be White: Money, Race, and God in America* (1999) demonstrates the central role played by shame in the formation of white identity.
3. UUA Commission on Appraisal, *Empowerment: One Denomination's Quest for Racial Justice, 1967–1982* (Boston: UUA, 1983).
4. Warren Ross, *The Premise and the Promise* (Boston: Skinner House, 2001).
5. Interview with William Jones, September 13, 2001.
6. Richard D. Leonard, *Call to Selma: Eighteen Days of Witness* (Boston: Skinner House, 2002).
7. Homer A. Jack, *Homer's Odyssey: My Quest for Peace and Justice* (Becket, MA: One Peaceful World Press, 1996), pp. 355–58.
8. James Luther Adams, "Our Unconquered Past," *Unitarian Christian*, Fall 1967, p. 4.
9. Homer A. Jack, "Towards Understanding the Black Rebellion: Some Personal Observations" (Boston: UUA Department of Social Responsibility, 1968), p. 6.
10. Roy A. Ockert, quoted in Alicia McNary Forsey, ed., *In Their Own Words: A Conversation with Participants in the Black Empowerment Movement within the Unitarian Universalist Association* (Berkeley, CA: Starr King School for the Ministry, 2001), pp. 61–64.
11. *Ibid.*, p. 62.
12. Jack, *Homer's Odyssey*, p. 354.
13. Jeannette Hopkins et al., *Special Report: Emergency Conference of the UU Response to the Black Rebellion: Proceedings* (Boston: UUA, 1967), p. 5.
14. Judge Wade McCree Jr., "Religion: Race and Reason," sermon, location unspecified, January 28, 1968.
15. *Ibid.*
16. Henry Hampton, "Last Exit to Grosse Pointe," *Respond* (published by the Laymen's League) Vol. 1, Fall 1967, p. 11.

17. Hopkins et al., *Special Report*, p. 31.
18. Martin Luther King, Jr., *Where Do We Go From Here: Chaos or Community* (New York: Harper & Row, 1967), p. 10.
19. Hampton, "Last Exit to Grosse Pointe," p. 33.
20. Robert Jones, "Reflections on the Black Caucus," *Respond* Vol. 2, No. 3, Winter 1968, p. 9.
21. Jack Mendelsohn, "Black Power and the Liberal Church," sermon, Arlington Street Church, Boston, November 5, 1967.
22. UUA Commission on Appraisal, *Empowerment*, p. 102.
23. *Ibid.*

Chapter 2

BURR, BUUC, BAC, FULLBAC, BAWA:
The Issue of Leadership

Almost from the moment of its creation at the Emergency Conference on the Black Rebellion in New York City in October 1967, the Black Unitarian Universalist Caucus came under attack by both white and black Unitarian Universalists. The Caucus's opponents believed that a caucus was unnecessary, and that its methods—secrecy, separatism, the demand for group solidarity among caucus members, and the demand that the Emergency Conference give unreserved acceptance and endorsement of the Caucus's proposals—were totally out of keeping with the principles of a free religious faith, undemocratic and alien to the Unitarian Universalist tradition. Furthermore, the Caucus's opponents perceived it as a threat to racial harmony, interpreting its endorsement of separatism as a repudiation of the quest for integration.

What these critics failed to perceive was that if individual black persons were to come to grips with their role as second-class citizens in this society—if they were to confront their blackness as a fundamental component affecting their human condition—that task had to be accomplished in the exclusive presence of other black people. The middle-class black Unitarian Universalists who assembled at the Biltmore Hotel in New York City faced a common dilemma: being members of two societies simultaneously, uncomfortable in both and fully accepted in neither.

The Caucus offered the first opportunity within the denomination for middle-class black Unitarian Universalists to come to terms with their blackness. It also served to focus the attention of middle-class black Unitarian Universalists on their relationship with the black underclass and their responsibility to assist that underclass, not as the emissaries of white largesse, but on the basis of their own decision-making capabilities. As Caucus member Henry Hampton observed, "the time has come to tell our liberal friends what we want and stop listening to what they want to do for us."[1]

The central and fundamental issue was the issue of black leadership and white trust, support, understanding, and affirmation of the need of blacks to exercise that leadership. Likewise, total and unequivocal commitment to black leadership meant accepting and unequivocally supporting of the Caucus proposals, including the financial demand for $250,000 each year for four years. In retrospect, it is clear that this level of commitment was indeed the only real commitment, as the Caucus members argued at the time.

One participant in the Emergency Conference debate was the Rev. Duke Gray, then Associate Minister at the First Church in Brooklyn. Gray had worked directly with the black community at a store-front outreach church in Brooklyn. He voiced the most cogent reason why the Caucus proposals should be accepted as stated, without further debate or amendment: "We have been asking the black people in our midst to uncritically endorse our liberal principles for years by their very presence in our churches; now it is our turn to show reciprocal faith, by investing ourselves unequivocally in what they have democratically determined is right for them."[2]

Gray's bold and perceptive endorsement spoke directly to the central issue of the Emergency Conference and, indeed, to much of what would transpire over the next months: who would lead? The issue of leadership would reveal much of what was hidden within the middle-class ideology of Unitarian Universalism: paternalism and unacknowledged, largely unconscious superiority and condescension. It would reveal a middle-class denomination's tendency to debate procedures for acting, rather than (and often as a substitute for) taking action. On that particular issue,

Black Caucus member Barbara Jackson would confront the Emergency Conference: "You fall back on your philosophical clichés, your parliamentary procedures. Can't you understand what we're trying to do? Can't you for once in your lives look past your own selves and see that what these people are trying to do is right and say: 'I will support them uncritically'?"[3]

The deeper, more pervasive, and more stubborn issue that the Caucus leadership would address was systemic racism. In the course of the next months and years, white Unitarian Universalists would learn a good deal about racism. We would learn that our easy equation of racism with discrimination was highly inadequate. White middle-class Unitarian Universalists had a long history of dealing with discrimination, or the actualization of feelings of racial prejudice. We had criticized and acted to overcome "racial discrimination" in places like Selma and Montgomery, Alabama.

But systemic racism was something that we would learn about. We would learn that even those who had worked assiduously for civil rights, who had worked to create interracial Unitarian Universalist committees and commissions, would be called "racist." We would learn that doing things with black people as a way of doing things *for* black people is racist; that paternalism is racist; that interracial committees established to bring about racial justice but which have white majorities are racist; that the very motive for helping a people, stemming from the knowledge that you are in a position of power which can be used to help them, is racist. We would learn that always being in a position of power and authority because of your race leads, inevitably, to an attitude of implicit or explicit superiority, which is racist. Leadership in confronting and challenging the issue of systemic racism, both within ourselves as a church and in the society in general, was central to the struggle that would grip us as a denomination for the next several years.

Denominational Responses to Black Demands

Less than a month after the Emergency Conference, the Unitarian Universalist Commission on Religion and Race, which had been organized by the Unitarian Universalist General Assembly in 1963, considered the Conference's recommendation that a Black Affairs Council be created. At this time the Commission was chaired by Community Church leader Cornelius McDougald, a black who had refused an invitation to join the Black Unitarian Universalist Caucus, saying that he would not participate in any group run by dictatorial demands.[4] After lengthy discussion and debate, the Commission affirmed its previous goals of a racially inclusive church and denomination, while calling for "a mature and positive" response to the Black Unitarian Universalist Caucus.[5]

The meeting of the UUA Board of Trustees on Nov. 12, 1967 was stormy. According to one observer, the discussion of the Emergency Conference recommendations proceeded "in the atmosphere of articulate positions, angles of vision, support, denunciations, tensions, ego structures, emotional personal involvements."[6]

Prior to presenting its recommendations to the Board, the Caucus asked that those recommendations receive either a positive or negative response before the end of the meeting—a request that occasioned, in the words of Dana Greeley, "one of the most unfortunate 120 minutes in our history . . . it set both sides back six months or a year and drove a wedge between us instead of creating a sense of understanding and partnership."[7]

Behind the Black Caucus tactics lay the twin issues of leadership and trust. Was the UUA Board of Trustees prepared to permit power and control to pass beyond its authority? The answer was a resounding "No." The Board rejected the demand for the funding of a Black Affairs Council with $250 million dollars a year for four years; it also felt unable to comply immediately with requests for changes in personnel and the racial restructuring of Unitarian Universalist committees. Instead, the Board passed what Greeley referred to as an "unimaginative motion" retooling the previously established and sanctioned Unitarian Universalist Commission on Religion and Race.[8]

Greeley tried to put the best possible face on this matter, saying that motion called for the Commission's reorganization "with the participation in this reorganization of the Steering Committee of the Black Caucus."[9] Unfortunately the motion itself does not bear Greeley out. It reads:

> As part of our effort to meet this challenge, we direct the reorganization of the commission on Religion and Race with the substantial participation of nonwhites and invite the participation of the Steering Committee of the Black Caucus to assist our churches and fellowships and the society of which we are a part.[10]

The Caucus Steering Committee was invited "to assist our churches and fellowships," not the Unitarian Universalist Commission on Religion and Race. Given the differing perspectives of the Caucus and the UU Commission, it could hardly have been otherwise.

Having refused to grant the request for funding, the Board's motion served to dismiss the Black Unitarian Universalist Caucus with faint encouragement to go out and provide some vague and unspecified assistance to Unitarian Universalist churches and fellowships. The members of the Black Caucus were disappointed. Black Caucus Steering Committee Chairperson Hayward Henry stated at a press conference shortly afterward that the Trustees' proposal for the Commission on Religion and Race was "too little and too late."[11] A careful reading of the Trustees' motion confirms Henry's charge that it reflected "a traditional racist and paternalistic approach to black problems."[12] Henry urged Unitarian Universalist churches and fellowships that wanted to combat racism in society to withhold financial support from the UUA and to contribute to the Black Unitarian Universalist Caucus.

In his paper describing the controversy, the Rev. Daniel Higgins asserts that "the essential point of difference [between the Caucus and the UUA] was the issue of separatism,"[13] quoting from a press release issued by Dana Greeley on November 13: "We (the Unitarian Universalist Association) will not honor and give funds to any group which is organized on purely racial lines. The Board has not abridged this liberal principle for either blacks or whites."[14]

But, in fact, there was no mention of separatism in the Caucus demands. On the contrary, the Caucus had asked to be recognized as an affiliate body of the UUA and had requested funds to develop programs in the name of Unitarian Universalism. It is hard to escape the conclusion that the charge of "separatism" was a bogus issue, invoked as a means of avoiding the real issues of leadership in the Unitarian Universalist response to systemic racism in both this liberal denomination and the country at large.

The UUA Board's rejection of the Caucus provoked an emphatic response from the First Unitarian Church of Los Angeles, where BURR had originated. Both the Board of Trustees and the congregation of First Unitarian adopted a resolution supporting the establishment of a Unitarian Universalist Black Affairs Council and urging denominational recognition of such an organization. In his letter to the UUA Board of Trustees, the Rev. Roy Ockert, wrote as follows:

> We white Unitarian Universalists who are proud of our denomination can take further pride in the desire of our black colleagues to remain Unitarian Universalists and in their expressed trust in our being able to recognize today's reality despite ancient principles that are no longer relevant to the human relations situation. The special circumstances of black Americans make ethnic organizations necessary and inevitable. The Black Affairs Council would make possible a greatly enhanced involvement of black people in the affairs of our denomination at all levels and through them and with them we will all be working more effectively for freedom for both black and white people.[15]

The first National Conference of the Black Unitarian Universalist Caucus occurred in Chicago on February 23–25, 1968. The Unitarian Universalist Commission on Religion and Race voted $4,100 from the UUA's Freedom Fund to help subsidize this national meeting. Two hundred seven black Unitarian Universalists attended; 203 were official delegates. Participants came from every region of the country, with large delegations from Boston, MA, southern California, and the Chicago area. (The Arlington Street Church appropriated $1,200 in travel expenses for Boston-area blacks to attend.) The conference had been called "to determine the relevancy of a predominantly white institution to its black constituency."[16] At the National Caucus, the feeling of racial solidarity that

Caucus members had experienced at the Emergency Conference in New York City was broadened and extended. The National Caucus produced three substantive decisions:

1. To create a Black Affairs Council to replace the Unitarian Universalist Association Commission on Religion and Race. The Caucus claimed the authority to do this themselves, without consulting with the UUA.
2. To present the general outline of a program to empower black communities to the Cleveland General Assembly in May 1968, along with the funding request for $250,000 a year for four years.
3. To make the National Caucus a permanent entity: the Black Unitarian Universalist Caucus (BUUC), a continuing body that would meet annually.[17] This was the first use of the BUUC acronym.

The National Caucus voted to collaborate with white sympathizers in examining white racism. They also recognized some of their white co-religionists as allies, including those grouped together in the Los Angeles-based organization Supporters of Black Unitarian Universalists for Radical Reform (SOBURR) and in what Homer Jack identified at the time as a national group apparently forming.[18]

Black Unitarians for Radical Reform (BURR) had been born at the First Unitarian Church of Los Angeles, and it is not surprising that SOBURR, the first demonstration of organized white support for BURR, should have originated here too, or that white Unitarian Universalists desiring to support the black agenda should look to the church for leadership. In early February 1968, Ann Raynolds, a member of the Arlington Street Church and leader of FULLBAC, wrote to the Rev. Roy Ockert asking for guidance in the establishment of a national white support network for BUUC and its agenda. She wrote:

> I believe the formation of a White Radical Caucus in support of Black interests within the denomination should be organized as soon as possible. As I see it the "issue" is being brought to focus in a microcosm of the total socie-

ty. How or if whites respond will blaze a trail for white response in the society as a whole.[19]

The letter is prophetic in its perception of the need for solidarity with blacks affirming black leadership. Raynolds continues:

> Serious thought must also be given and support solicited among whites for a walkout (from the denomination) with blacks if and when *they* decide that time has come. If our organization known as the Unitarian Universalist Association should split, it should not be along black and white lines. This *type* of solidarity might save Unitarianism from racism (white and black would leave *together*) and it would present a guide for action as the society as a whole confronts the issue under far less favorable and controlled conditions.[20]

One observer has noted that "the month before the Unitarian Universalist General Assembly at Cleveland, a group of Unitarian Universalists formed FULLBAC (Full Recognition and Funding for the Black Affairs Council)."[21] But this was not the first group to support the black demands. The fact is that as early as December 1967, only two months after the Emergency Conference in New York City, SOBURR had issued its statement of purpose: "to support as strongly and as effectively as we can the proposals of the Black Caucus."[22] By the time the National Black Caucus was formed in February 1968, SOBURR was prepared to support the Caucus's specific recommendations and help to organize a nationwide network of white support.

Thus, even as the Unitarian Universalist Association Board was reacting against BUUC, white Unitarian Universalists were mobilizing themselves to support its aims. The Emergency Conference had moved white as well as black Unitarian Universalists to identify and act against the corrosive effects of systemic racism and the middle-class ideology that sheltered and masked its effects upon denomination and society.

In March 1968 the National Advisory Commission on Civil Disorders, which had been appointed by President Lyndon B. Johnson, published an important report. The massive evidence the Commission had compiled pointed to one basic conclusion: "Our nation is moving toward two societies, one black, one white—separate and unequal."[23] The report was addressed essentially to white society. The black community needed no Commission report to instruct it in this truth.

Within a week of the appearance of the National Advisory Commission's report, SOBURR distributed a circular to ministers and denominational leaders calling attention to the report's emphasis on white racism. The circular reaffirmed support for the formation of a Unitarian Universalist Black Affairs Council as an affiliate agency of the UUA and called for a network alliance of groups and persons sharing this point of view. Leona H. Light of Beverly Hills, California, the Secretary of SOBURR, and Ann Raynolds of Springfield, Vermont were both designated "temporary co-chairmen" of this new organization in company with the Rev. David B. Parke of Philadelphia and the Rev. Jack Mendelsohn of Boston. The organization would be known by its acronym, FULLBAC.

FULLBAC, created "to mobilize support at the Unitarian Universalist Association General Assembly in Cleveland to secure recognition and adequate funding of the Black Affairs Council"[24] and seeking national participation and support, was welcomed by SOBURR. In a letter to Hayward Henry of BAC, the SOBURR executive committee had gone on record saying "it did not think that a national set-up should be imposed from Southern California."[25] By mid-March, FULLBAC had issued a statement mobilizing support for the Black Affairs Council agenda to be presented at the General Assembly in Cleveland. Affirming black leadership and participatory democracy, the statement affirmed the black revolution as giving Unitarian Universalists "the freedom to explore radical alternatives to a society that denies its children, murders its heroes, and turns a dream to dust. . . ."[26]

The first meeting of the FULLBAC steering committee occurred in Philadelphia over the weekend of April 4, 1968—the date of Martin Luther King, Jr.'s assassination. Representatives of BUUC and BAC were present at the meeting, which was in progress when the announcement of the assassination was made. Almost as if by pre-arrangement, black and white Unitarian Universalists separated. They would not come together until the pain of their grief had eased and they could return to the common cause of black empowerment. Still, in less than a month, FULLBAC was able to publish a list of initial sponsors representing churches and fellowships across the continent. The list began with the name of Professor James Luther Adams and included Dr. Homer Jack, then the director of the UUA Department of Social Responsibility.

Meanwhile, back at 25 Beacon Street, the UUA Board of Trustees continued to struggle with the issues growing out of the Emergency Conference. The Board had been subjected to a series of attacks from BUUC and its supporters, articulating strong disapproval of the statement made by the Board at its November 1967 meeting, in particular the Board's decision to reorganize the Commission on Religion and Race.

At its January 1968 meeting, the UUA Board received a letter from Black Caucus Chairperson Hayward Henry asking that the reorganization of the Commission be delayed until after the National Caucus meeting scheduled to be held in Chicago in February. The Board agreed to postpone its decision, although it did accept the resignations of the Commission's members.[27]

By March 1968, the Board was faced with the fact that the National Caucus of Black Unitarian Universalists had established a Black Affairs Council at its Chicago meeting. Whereas in November the UUA Board had declined to make any official statement concerning the formation of the Black Unitarian Universalist Caucus, by March the Board was prepared somewhat reluctantly to acknowledge that the emergence of the Caucus had been beneficial to the denomination and to welcome the formation of the Black Affairs Council.[28]

The UUA Board then turned its attention to reorganizing the Commission on Religion and Race, ignoring the express recommendation of the National Caucus that the Commission be abolished, since "it has not been relevant to Black needs."[29] The Caucus had also asserted that "it would not participate in the proposed reorganization of the Commission."[30] The Board acknowledged the achievements of the Commission on Religion and Race, asserted that its limitations were caused by "inadequate mandate and financing," and voted to establish, in place of the Commission, a Unitarian Universalist Commission for Action on Race.

The Board voted to establish this new Commission by April 1, 1968. It also voted to terminate the Unitarian Universalist Freedom Fund (which had been created in 1965) on June 30, 1968. It recommended that a new Unitarian Universalist "Fund for Racial Justice Now" be established with an annual goal of $300,000, to be administered by the newly established Commission. According to Homer Jack's report, "an attempt was made to indicate expressly that BAC would be one of the agencies receiving allocations, but this trial motion was defeated."[31]

It is relevant to ask why, having acknowledged the benefits to the denomination provided by the formation of the Black Caucus and having welcomed its application for affiliate membership status in the UUA, the UUA Board of Trustees should pursue the task of restructuring an instrumentality which the Caucus had charged with irrelevance. According to Homer Jack, "the rationale of the Administration and the Board for the establishment of this new Commission was chiefly that the Association could not forfeit its responsibility for organization and action in this field if it is indeed the highest denominational programmatic emphasis and the number one problem in the nation."[32]

Jack was putting the best possible face on what he personally perceived to be a bad situation. In a memo to President Greeley, written on the same date as his fact paper, Jack gave his initial reactions to the UUA Board's decisions. He argued that the Board had "opened a new wound" by suggesting that BAC's affiliate status might be questionable unless it was racially inclusive. Given that BAC from the beginning had indicated that it would be racially inclusive, with blacks in the majority, the UUA Board appeared in fact to be questioning the BAC Board's quotas of two-thirds black members, one-third white, as well as the fact that the "non-inclusive" BUUC nominated the BAC Board members.[33]

Jack also expressed reservations about the new Commission for Action on Race, which was not much different from the old Commission on Religion and Race, and about the new Fund for Racial Justice Now. As Jack notes, "the new Fund might well allocate large amounts to BAC, but this is not automatic, and BAC has no political leverage on the allocations of this Fund."[34]

Thus, the UUA had chosen to initiate a fund rather than acknowledging that BAC needed funds that *it controlled* in order to implement its program. Eventually, BUUC drew the conclusion that (in Hayward Henry's words) "White Power again wishes to co-opt the Black Movement, which is a traditional form of Liberal Racism."[35] There was nothing in the UUA Board's action to counter or seriously dispute that charge.

Jack foresaw that the Board's actions would come under severe attack from BUUC and its supporters. He predicted that the attack would culminate at the Unitarian Universalist General Assembly in Cleveland, at which time efforts would be made to (1) dissolve the Commission for Action on Race, (2) liquidate the Fund for Racial Justice Now, (3) obtain recognition of BAC, and (4) obtain denominational funds for BAC.[36] He was right on all counts.

As Jack had predicted, the Black Affairs Council, the Black Unitarian Universalist Caucus, and their white supporters viewed both the Board's actions and its rationale negatively. BAC and BUUC interpreted the UUA Board's refusal to cede responsibility as a refusal to acknowledge and support black leadership in dealing with "the number one problem in the nation." In a letter to Dr. Homer Jack, FULLBAC co-chair Ann Raynolds asserted that the establishment of the new Commission for Action on Race was "a very sophisticated ploy for subverting Black Caucus Leadership."[37] Raynolds was appalled at the spectacle of the Board's willingness—having reacted negatively to BUUC's proposal for funding at the rate of $250,000 a year for four years—to launch a new Unitarian Universalist Fund for Racial Justice with an annual goal of $300,000, to be administered by the Unitarian Universalist Commission, to which BAC might apply for funding.

The consternation and anger aroused by the UUA Board's new Commission for Action on Race reverberated through the pages of the Laymen's League magazine *Respond* and occasioned dissent within the Board itself.

One UUA Board member, the Rev. Mason McGinness, defended the Board's action and hinted that there was a conspiracy to undermine the

Board's efforts to establish the new Commission.[38] Responding to McGinness's letter, board member Carleton Fisher acknowledged that the Board may very well have "hoisted itself with its own petard." Having welcomed BAC and indicated a willingness to grant it affiliate membership, Fisher said,

> we proceed to do two things that fly in the face of this recognition. (1) We go out of our way to say the BAC must be racially inclusive and not totally black, because our constitution and by-laws so demand; and (2) we proceed to downgrade BAC's importance by indicating that it will be but one of a number of Unitarian Universalist agencies who may be funded out of a new Fund for Racial Justice Now to be administered by a brand new Commission for Action on Race, which will be racially inclusive. What all this says, of course, is that we of the 98% white majority insist on calling the shots; and we will not, in fact, give any decision making powers to the black leadership.[39]

President Dana Greeley's reply to the McGinness letter was more conciliatory. Greeley said, "I have become somewhat more sympathetic or understanding, if that is a fair word, in relation to the nature of the Black Caucus. . . . I want new forces to flourish that will effect social change by peaceful means."[40] Greeley had become something of an apologist for the Caucus. "In a large number of speeches in the spring," he later wrote in his memoir, "I compared the blacks of the Black Caucus not only to young people who might rebel against their own families to achieve their identity and then join them later as coequals, and to a labor union organized for power purposes and insisting upon exclusive bargaining privileges, but also to the early woman suffragettes."[41] There is, however, a strong element of condescension in this supportive argument. While acknowledging that conditions of powerlessness and oppression do exist, and that persons have the right to struggle against them, there is little identification with the persons involved in the struggle and no indictment of the conditions which constitute their oppression.

35

Greeley had both sparked and led the denomination's response to social injustice in Selma, Alabama. His record as an advocate of civil rights was outstanding. Why, then, did Greeley choose to base his support for black empowerment on historical precedent rather than venture identification with those involved in the contemporary struggle? My judgment is that he felt more secure in citing historical examples of empowerment, and, more importantly, he knew that his personal identification with those seeking empowerment would provoke a counter-reaction so vehement as to compromise and render ineffective any leadership that he could provide to this increasingly divided denomination.

Less than a month before the General Assembly in Cleveland, Unitarian Universalists who had negative views about the Black Unitarian Universalist Caucus and the Black Affairs Council began to organize themselves. In a letter dated April 26, 1968 to Homer Jack, the Rev. Donald Harrington of the Community Church of New York expressed his indignation that Dr. Jack's Department of Social Responsibility was encouraging "a black-white confrontation which may very well end in a polarization of blacks and whites in the Denomination and make further integration far more difficult." Citing anthropologist Margaret Mead's support for "gradual integration of the educated Negro into all realms of the majority society," Harrington suggested the formation of an organization "Blacks And Whites Together, for a radical program."[42]

Replying to Harrington, Homer Jack wrote of his hope that "radical Blacks and Whites together" would be "what our whole denomination would become, with the Black Unitarian Universalist Caucus and now FULLBAC the radical sub-caucus within our total denomination, and working closely together."[43]

That was not what Harrington had in mind. He drew up and published a list of particulars about BUUC and BAC that, in his judgment, showed their contempt for and defiance of "the most fundamental liberal and democratic principles." Harrington charged the Caucus with being "a racially segregated organization"; that its "technique of presenting itself as a fait accompli by the action of a few individuals" and then claiming both to represent and speak for all or most Unitarian Universalist Blacks is subversive to the democratic process; that the proposed Black

36

Affairs Council, by definition two-thirds black and one-third white and controlled by the Black Caucus, "looks like a quota'd, tokenist front for the segregated Black Caucus" and that the demand for large amounts of money, "undesignated and unmatched to particular programs, is bad financial practice."[44]

To those who shared these doubts and uncertainties about BAC and BUUC, Donald Harrington and Cornelius McDougald, the black chair of the board of Community Church and the former chair of the Commission on Religion and Race, offered a carefully drawn prospectus of a new organization to be called Unitarian Universalists for a Black and White Alternative (BAWA). The stated purpose of BAWA was "to provide an independent denominational agency in which the black and white Unitarian Universalists, and those of all other races who desire to pursue a program of action for equality within the Unitarian Universalist Church and our American society at large, can work together as equals."[45]

The BAWA Prospectus was distributed nationwide two weeks before the General Assembly in Cleveland. It reflected the traditional philosophy of racial integration and articulated the themes associated with the Civil Rights Movement. Statements such as "We don't have to be black. We don't have to be white. We are free to be individual human beings united in a common human struggle to create a life of dignity and peace" discount racial difference as a factor in human relations, acclaiming individuality instead.[46] Not least among the appealing elements of such a statement is that it taps directly into the accepted and acceptable corpus of ideas which comprised the middle-class ideology of the denomination.

Speaking to a more radical segment of the denomination, FULLBAC co-chair the Rev. David Parke addressed the issue of racism directly: "Racism in America perpetuates injustice in the name of equality, exploitation in the name of impartiality, and segregation in the name of selectivity."[47] Parke was attacking not only racism but also the implicit assumptions of middle-class ideology. Thus were the issues and perspectives delineated on the eve of the Cleveland General Assembly in 1968.

Describing the emotional climate at the General Assembly, the Rev. Daniel Higgins has observed that "since October of 1967 Unitarian Universalists had debated separatism versus integration, principle versus expedience, gradualism versus revolution, black power versus black/white power, liberalism versus radicalism, ends versus means. Now the issue was joined. The agenda was set."[48] But Higgins has missed something. While each of the topics he names was indeed the subject of intense and often heated debate, the central issue to which each topic either pointed or sought to avoid was, Who would lead the Unitarian Universalist effort to overcome the corrosive and dehumanizing effects of systemic racism? The immediate issue at the heart of the debate was funding or refusing to fund BAC. These linked issues would occasion hours of debate among the 1350 delegates from the 364 Unitarian Universalist societies represented on the floor of the General Assembly.[49]

On the issue of funding both BAC and BAWA, BAC and its supporters were adamant. The UUA Board had recommended that BAWA be funded in addition to BAC.[50] The funds to be allocated to BAWA were meager in comparison to the funding which BAC was demanding. Funding BAWA, in my assessment, was an attempt by the Board to honor the principle of pluralism. BAC and FULLBAC, however, perceived it as yet another ploy in the ongoing effort to deflect the denomination away from committing itself to black leadership. BAC and FULLBAC spokespersons addressed the Assembly declaring that if BAWA received any official denominational funding at all, BAC would refuse funding on the grounds that the integrationist approach represented by BAWA was incompatible with, and could only be interpreted as an attempt to undermine and subvert, the leadership of blacks, which BAC represented. The proposal to fund BAWA was defeated by the General Assembly delegates. On the afternoon of Sunday, May 26, in the emotionally charged atmosphere of the General Assembly, the motion to adopt the resolution proposed by the Black Affairs Council was moved, voted, and carried by a vote of 836 to 326.[51]

Thus the General Assembly delegates had catapulted their denomination into a position of unchallenged leadership among all the religious bodies on this continent who were concerned with issues of black empowerment.

The motion for a fully-funded, fully-recognized BAC passed by a majority in excess of 70% of the voting delegates. That vote accomplished four things: (1) it fulfilled the promise made by the Unitarian Universalist presence in Selma, Alabama, that the Unitarian Universalists were serious in demanding a denominational commitment to black empowerment; (2) it demonstrated the power of the Unitarian Universalist laity, both black and white, organized and working together in cooperation to lead the denomination in the area of race relations; (3) it gave the nation its first example of a denomination's making a significant "reparational" response to the conditions of racism in America, identifying race relations as the prime domestic problem and demanding that this conviction be reflected in budget and programs; and (4) it accepted and affirmed black Unitarian Universalist leadership.

Reporting on the controversy in *The Christian Century*, Homer Jack wrote that "thanks to the Black Caucus, Unitarian Universalism will never be the same again."[52] Jack was correct that these changes were revolutionary but faulty in his judgments concerning the locus of these changes. He believed the change was occurring in the denominational hierarchy. "Certainly," he wrote, "this controversy will determine the kind of persons elected in the future to the Board of Trustees and to the Presidency, as well as the kind of programs in which the local churches engage."[53] In fact, however, the changes occurred not at the hierarchical top of the denomination but at the grass roots, where youth, women, gays, and the aging would demand and claim the power to make decisions affecting their welfare and direct the denomination to accept their leadership in everything that concerned them.

But black Unitarian Universalists would never again receive such an endorsement as that given at the Cleveland General Assembly on May 26, 1968. Unitarian Universalist black empowerment had achieved its greatest measure of denominational acceptance and support. In future weeks and months, the middle-class ideology would reassert itself with a virulence of astonishing ferocity.

Notes

1. Henry Hampton, "An Insider's View of the Black Caucus," *Special Report: The UU Black Caucus Controversy* (Boston: UUA, 1968), p. 24.

2. *Ibid.*, p. 25.

3. Henry Hampton, "Last Exit to Grosse Pointe," *Respond*, Vol. 1, Fall 1967, p. 15.

4. *Ibid.* p. 12.

5. Minutes of the UU Commission on Race and Religion, November 4, 1967.

6. Daniel G. Higgins, Jr., "The UUA Color Line Controversy (1967–1969): Theological Implications," paper presented at Collegium, Craigville, MA, October 1979, p. 7.

7. Dana Greeley, *25 Beacon Street and Other Recollections* (Boston: Skinner House, 1971), p. 113.

8. *Ibid.*

9. Minutes of the UUA Board of Trustees, November 12, 1967.

10. *Boston Herald Traveler,* November 14, 1967.

11. *Boston Globe,* November 14, 1967.

12. Higgins, "The UUA Color Line Controversy," p. 8.

13. *Ibid.*

14. *Ibid.*

15. Roy Ockert, letter to UUA Board of Trustees, December 1967.

16. "The National Caucus of Black Unitarian Universalists: A Preliminary Report from a Non-Participant" (memo), February 29, 1968, p. 1.

17. *Ibid.* p. 2.

18. Homer Jack, "Introduction," in Jeannette Hopkins et al., *Special Report: Emergency Conference of the UU Response to the Black Rebellion: Proceedings* (Boston: UUA, 1967), p. 2.

19. Ann Raynolds, letter to Roy Ockert, February 4, 1968.

20. *Ibid.*

21. Higgins, "The UUA Color Line Controversy," p. 9.

22. SOBURR, Statement of Purpose, December 1967.

23. Otto Kerner et al., *Report of the National Advisory Commission on Civil Disorders* (New York: Bantam, 1968), p. 1.

24. David B. Parke, letter to Rudolf Gelsey, March 22, 1968.

25. Leona Light, letter to Hayward Henry, March 12, 1968.

26. FULLBAC, "Cleveland and Beyond: A Summons to Unitarian Universalists," April 1968, p. 11.

27. Minutes of the UUA Board of Trustees, January 23, 1968.

28. Homer Jack, "The UUA Board and The Black Caucus" (mimeographed fact paper), March 17, 1968.

29. *Ibid.*

30. *Ibid.*

31. *Ibid.*

32. *Ibid.*

33. Homer Jack, letter to Dana Greeley, March 17, 1968.

34. *Ibid.*

35. Hayward Henry, sermon delivered at First Unitarian Church of Newton, MA,

March 1968.

36. Homer Jack, letter to Dana Greeley, March 17, 1968.

37. Ann Raynolds, letter to Homer Jack, March 22, 1968.

38. Mason McGinness, letter to UUA Board of Trustees, May 6, 1968.

39. Carleton N. Fisher, letter to UUA Board of Trustees, May 10, 1968.

40. Dana McLean Greeley, letter to Mason McGinness, May 9, 1968.

41. Greeley, *25 Beacon Street*, p. 117.

42. Donald Harrington, letter to Homer Jack, April 26, 1968.

43. Homer Jack, letter to Donald Harrington, April 29, 1968.

44. Leslie Pennington, notes on a sermon delivered by Donald Harrington at First Unitarian Church of Newton, MA, May 18, 1968.

45. BAWA Prospectus (Oakland, CA).

46. *Ibid.*

47. "UU Views of Black-White Relations" (pamphlet) (Boston: UUA, 1968), p. 10.

48. Higgins, "The UUA Color Line Controversy," p. 10.

49. *1969 Directory* (Boston: UUA Board of Trustees, 1968).

50. Minutes of the UUA Board of Trustees, May 23, 1968.

51. *1969 Directory*, p. 42.

52. Homer Jack, "Black Power Confronts Unitarian Universalists," *Christian Century*, June 26, 1968.

53. *Ibid.*

Chapter 3

"But Not Both":
An Ideology Strained to Its Limits

The Cleveland General Assembly had voted to fully fund the Black Affairs Council (BAC). Both this outcome and the process by which it had been achieved occasioned outcry and protest from elements within the denomination that were unsympathetic to the Black UU Caucus (BUUC), BAC, and FULLBAC (Full Recognition and Funding for the Black Affairs Council). Many within the denomination (and specifically within BAWA) questioned whether a denomination committed to the democratic process should ever vote its approval of "demands" which had, in effect, been dictated to it. There is no question that each stage of the development of the black empowerment controversy had been characterized by demands, often articulated in atmospheres of intentional effrontery. The tactics were engendered in part by desperation, in part by insecurity, in part by contempt for white liberal gentility and its capacity to obfuscate issues.

The growth and development of BUUC and BAC from the Biltmore Conference to Cleveland can be read as a studied attempt to humble the proud and to certify a new pride in those who had long been humbled. The central issue—who would exercise leadership in the denomination's response to the black revolution?—could and occasionally did become obscured by the conflict of pride versus pride. FULLBAC, the white support group, answered this question most satisfactorily by pointing out that pride is a two-edged sword rendering a curse "on both houses," but the pride of the strong and powerful is more destructive than the pride of the weak. Pointing out that our liberal religious tradition had historically condemned the arrogance of sanctified power, the FULLBAC leadership steadfastly maintained that the issue of black leadership should not be deflected and diverted in order to address the relatively minor concern of the abrasive character of the demands.

A more serious dilemma centered on the question of using racial classification for financial benefit, especially in a denomination that had historically designated racism as a principal enemy and honored racial equality as a cherished value and social goal.

Addressing this dilemma in a broad context, Mark Green, editor of the *Harvard Civil Rights–Civil Liberties Review,* produced the cogent argument that, where 40.6% of nonwhites lived in poverty compared with 11.9% of whites, 7% of blacks were unemployed or underemployed compared with 3% of whites, and the average black family income was 58% of that of whites, and falling, it was surely possible to distinguish between racial classification for good and for evil. Further, there were all kinds of preferential classifications already operating that *de jure* or *de facto* excluded blacks. Therefore "preferential treatment seeks, rather than avoids or opposes, the goal of racial equality."[1]

Meeting in Boston in June 1968, the UUA Board of Trustees struggled to reconcile recognition of BAC with its own bylaws. UUA General Counsel Frank Frederick pointed out that the UUA Constitution read in part, "Each affiliate member shall in respect of its work refrain from the practice of segregation based on race or color" (Article III, Section 7, Rule 4).[2] After considerable debate, the Unitarian Universalist Association Board voted to modify Rule 4 by adding a clause:

> This rule is not intended to preclude those affiliates designed to benefit special interest groups whose past exclusion from the larger society warrants organizing around a "special interest" of race and color, in order to insure fuller participation in the total society.[3]

The UUA Board encountered no such difficulty in granting affiliate status to BAWA, which, by that time, had changed its full name from "Black and White Alternative" to "Black and White Action" in order to de-emphasize its original purpose of providing an alternative to BUUC.

Daniel Higgins has characterized the year between the General Assembly in Cleveland and the General Assembly in Boston as follows: "As fall gave way to winter, what had begun as a 'Response to the Black Rebellion and gave way to the 'Black Controversy' now became the BAC/BAWA Controversy."[4] I suggest, however, that this nomenclature seriously distorts and obscures the nature of the denominational struggle with the issue of black empowerment. The pairing of BAC and BAWA elevates BAWA to a place of unwarranted importance while shifting the focus away from the challenge which BUUC/BAC continued to present to the denomination. Such pairing creates the false impression that BAC and BAWA were equal contenders in an isolated issue on the periphery of denominational consciousness. This in turn provides the option for those not deeply engaged with the issues of black empowerment to view a so-called "BAC/BAWA Controversy" as something remote from them, which might well invite the exasperated response, "We've had enough of this race issue; let us get on with our denominational business!" In fact, "our business" was to deal with the issues that empowerment (represented by BUUC/BAC) had forced the denomination to confront. Black empowerment did not call for assimilation of black persons into a white society but for the creation of a new society enjoying historical and cultural contributions from both blacks and whites, a society to which both races would bring their traditions and values, each receiving from the other.

The vote at the Cleveland General Assembly established BUUC/BAC as leaders of the Unitarian Universalist response to the black revolution going on in American society and pace-setters for the wider religious community. BAWA, for all the civil rights credentials of its leadership, never overcame its initial motivation: a fearful reaction to black leadership taking denominational power away from white control.

The "BAC/BAWA controversy" nomenclature also obscures the profoundly important successes and failures in the development of new models of black/white cooperation, and the effective social change resulting from that cooperation. A significant example of this cooperation is the efforts of the Boston chapters of BUUC and FULLBAC to change the discriminatory hiring practices of the Boston Statler Hilton Hotel, which was scheduled to house the Boston General Assembly in July 1969.

BUUC and FULLBAC members felt that the UUA, "historically and publicly a supporter of civil rights, should financially support only those institutions which concur in practice with the Unitarian Universalist view of the equality and dignity of all."[5] As the Boston branch of BUUC discovered, the Statler Hilton's hiring practices were not in line with this view. In November 1968, Boston BUUC approached Boston FULLBAC requesting that FULLBAC examine these hiring practices. This was a totally appropriate way to handle the inquiry, since FULLBAC was the group working to eliminate racism.

A series of meetings with the hotel management stretched over the next seven months leading up to the General Assembly, involving Homer Jack (UUA Department of Social Responsibility), Virginia Mulley (UUA General Assembly Coordinator), the Massachusetts Commission Against Discrimination, and representatives of other civil rights organizations, as well as Hilton personnel and representatives of FULLBAC. Despite some resistance on the part of the hotel staff, the final changes in hiring practices were sufficiently positive that the General Assembly was held at the hotel as originally scheduled.[6]

These events were also significant as a model of cooperation between Boston BUUC and Boston FULLBAC, which instigated the hotel hiring changes. Boston BUUC was committed to expanding employment opportunities for black people; Boston FULLBAC was committed to counteracting the patterns of institutional racism perpetuated by white people. Boston FULLBAC was sufficiently organized to be able to act on its own, using the resources of its own people and exerting its own power. BUUC acknowledged and respected this degree of organization in FULLBAC. When a coalition of forces was needed to meet the hotel's resistance, BUUC could rely upon FULLBAC's determination and joined FULLBAC in coalition. In this situation FULLBAC was able to act on its own initiative and not simply to respond to BUUC's directive, thus strengthening itself organizationally.

Thus, the Statler Hilton inquiry provides a full-fledged example not only of FULLBAC supporting BUUC, but of BUUC supporting FULL-BAC, a model of cooperation in which organized blacks and organized whites each determined their own agendas and came together at the points where their mutual self-interest could be enhanced by joining forces. In the BUUC/FULLBAC model, each separate entity works functionally on its own behalf. Such a model of cooperation differs markedly from the BAWA approach, in which work is done on another's behalf.

Within the restricted context of the Statler Hilton inquiry, the BUUC/FULLBAC model of cooperating organizations worked well. Under the extreme pressure of time and circumstance created by the 1969 General Assembly, however, that model would founder.

During the year since the Cleveland vote, the movement to fund BAC had been accelerating both within and beyond the denomination. Jeremy Taylor, then the Unitarian Universalist Service Committee Director of Domestic Programs, characterized the deep division within the denomination accurately:

> At its deepest level, it is a disagreement between the large and growing number of Unitarian Universalists who cannot contain their anxiety, anger, and frustration over the direction of the Unitarian Universalist Association and the country as a whole, and those other Unitarian Universalists who, although they have an uneasy sense that things are not what they should be, are still convinced that there is nothing inherently wrong that a little bit more talk, money and good will wouldn't take care of.[7]

These two forces—profoundly felt but only dimly understood—would meet head-on at the eighth General Assembly, gathered in Boston in July 1969.

The UUA administration and the UUA Board of Trustees both *really?* understood the financial squeeze on the denominational budget represented by the Cleveland General Assembly vote to fund BAC at $250,000

47

per year for four years. Both Homer Jack and President Dana Greeley
have acknowledged the debates at denominational headquarters on this
issue, including attempts to evade the General Assembly directive on the
matter by, for example, spreading payments out over a five-year rather
than a four-year period. Acknowledging that such a proposal was unacceptable to BAC, the UUA Board diverged in another way from the
Cleveland General Assembly vote to fund BAC for four years, deciding
that the BAC appropriation would need to be re-affirmed and voted
annually at each subsequent General Assembly. BUUC/BAC and
FULLBAC were dismayed. They charged that the denomination's leadership had failed to honor and uphold the commitment to black
empowerment which had been made at the Cleveland General
Assembly. From the BUUC/BAC and FULLBAC point of view, the
new vote on BAC funding on the Boston General Assembly agenda violated the Cleveland commitment.

To this perceived insult was added the injury of the printed agenda,
which would occasion the first clash of the Assembly.

The final printed agenda, produced by the UUA Business Committee
and distributed to the delegates before the Assembly began, followed the
established pattern. The delegates would not be given the option of
deciding for or against the Business Committee's recommendation of full
funding for BAC plus $50,000 for BAWA until days after the Assembly
had been convened.

Some delegates, who had labored for months to organize support
for BUUC/BAC, and were filled with an urgent sense that history was
confronting the denomination, were incensed by what they perceived to
be subversive tactics behind the 'business as usual" approach of the
printed agenda.

In a sermon delivered at the Arlington Street Church on the day
before the General Assembly began, the Reverend Jack Mendelsohn
called for a new ordering of agenda priorities. Acknowledging the historic
nature of the moment and the high emotional energy of delegates,
Mendelsohn poured scorn upon the printed agenda and its makers, who
were, in Mendelsohn's words, inviting the delegates "to graze like con-
tented sheep on pastures of printed matter."[8]

On Monday, immediately after the Official Business Session was called to order, BAC and FULLBAC offered an alternative "rules of procedure" to the Assembly, which would have placed the funding issue at the beginning of the agenda. The vote to accept the alternative gained a simple majority of the votes (710 for, 536 against) but fell short of the two-thirds majority vote required.[9] BAC chairperson Hayward Henry addressed the Assembly and declared, "Unless the Assembly agrees to deal with these basic problems (the funding of BAC and BAWA) now and not next Wednesday, the microphones will be possessed and the business of this house will come to a halt."[10]

By prearrangement a member of BUUC stood at each of the Assembly floor microphones in order to prevent any delegates from addressing the Assembly. In addition to being dramatic and abrasive, the act of "possessing" the Assembly microphones was highly symbolic. Black Unitarian Universalists were symbolically in control of the four Assembly "avenues of power." Their controlling presence was a profound demonstration of the frustration that results when people are denied access to power. Thus were the delegates to the Eighth General Assembly of the UUA invited to experience the feelings of BUUC/BAC.

Totally unused to such tactics, the delegates reacted with consternation and outrage. So angry were they that, in the main, they did not perceive or consciously register another fact that was as noteworthy as the microphone "possession": at each of the "captured" microphones stood not only a member of BUUC but also a representative of the Continental Liberal Religious Youth. Unitarian Universalist blacks and Unitarian Universalist youth had made common cause, symbolized by their common presence at the Assembly microphones and based on their perception of a common adversary: middle-class ideology, with its components of racism and militarism.

I have already noted how blacks, even middle-class Unitarian Universalist blacks, felt the oppressive force exerted by the implicit and explicit tenets of middle-class ideology. Youth, even middle-class Unitarian Universalist youth, also experienced that same ideology as oppressive, as it sanctioned and encouraged their removal to Vietnam. Martin Luther King, Jr., a year before his assassination, had identified a linkage between racism and imperialism. Standing with Unitarian Universalist blacks at the Assembly microphones, Unitarian Universalist youth were identifying the source of their own oppression as the prevailing ideology whose "business-as-usual" facade obscured the harsh realities visited upon those whom the powerful and secure designated as expendable.

The symbolic nature of the microphone "possession" was lost on the Assembly delegates. It did, however, show them that the central and pivotal issue of the Assembly—the question of funding BAC or BAWA—was an either-or choice.

At his next opportunity to speak, Hayward Henry addressed the issue of the Unitarian Universalist Association Board of Trustees' recommendation proposing two allocations ($250,000 to BAC and $50,000 to BAWA).

Hayward Henry told the Assembly that it had to choose between the two allocations: "You can fund BAC, or BAWA . . . *but not both!*" "If the funding of BAWA is voted," said Henry, "BAC will accept nothing." He continued, "We [BAC] have been telling the Unitarian Universalist Association Board of Trustees this for nine months and nothing has been done to correct the situation. What we seek is a reparational grant, which is our due, by the 1968 vote."[11] Henry's statement reflects BAC's awareness that the UUA Board of Trustees, not BAWA, was its adversary. By recommending funding for BAWA, the Board had distracted the Assembly from the Board's failure to honor the Cleveland General Assembly directive that the denomination fund BAC for four years. The UUA Board had shifted attention away from its own actions by bringing up the liberal doctrine of fairness and the principle of pluralism.

Reflecting on the principle of pluralism, Homer Jack's perceptions are instructive:

> If only as a corrective, pluralism (social and theological) is one hallmark of our denomination. If there are whites and/or Blacks (Negroes) who believe in the BAWA approach, they have every legitimacy in our denomination. I am glad BAWA was recognized by the Board a year ago and given, together with BAC, associate member status.

> But pluralism does not automatically mean that the
> denominational budget must subsidize both organiza-
> tions, or in equal amounts.[12]

While Jack's explication of pluralism and its place within liberal religion is apt as regards the issue of funding, it distracts from the basic and fundamental issue of leadership: Who would lead the Unitarian Universalist response to the black revolution?

The "reparational" allocation to BAC at Cleveland and BAC's subsequent programmatic thrusts were demonstrating to the larger black community that BAC (and, by extension, the Unitarian Universalists) could provide effective leadership to the black community generally, even though BUUC/BAC was a part of a white establishment organization. In order to maintain its effectiveness in the black community, particularly with militant blacks, BUUC/BAC had to prove that the UUA was committed to black empowerment. The best evidence of this commitment was funding BUUC/BAC.

But if, in addition to funding BAC, the UUA was to vote funds for BAWA and its integrationist approach, which had been discredited by the black community at the heart of the black revolution, BAC would appear to have been compromised by the white establishment and would lose its credibility as a leader of the black militant movement for social change.

Thus was BAC struggling on two fronts simultaneously. It needed to maintain its credibility with the black community, which looked to it for leadership, while, at the same time, it tried to keep the denomination focused on and committed to its efforts, which it made in the name of Unitarian Universalism and which depended on Unitarian Universalist dollars.

The Monday business session of the General Assembly ended with nothing resolved. On Tuesday morning another motion was made to alter the agenda so that the black agenda could be dealt with before any other business came before the Assembly. The depth and breadth of division among the delegates can be measured by the vote on this issue. The motion to reconsider lost by a vote of 692 to 687, a difference of only five votes.[13] A motion to recount was tabled. The printed agenda would be followed; the established order had triumphed. Without fanfare or ceremony, BUUC walked out of the Assembly.

As the Assembly turned to the scheduled business of presidential candidates presenting their views, members of FULLBAC met with members of BUUC/BAC in the BUUC/BAC hotel suite. Returning to the Assembly as the candidates were concluding their remarks, Jack Mendelsohn and other FULLBAC members came to the speakers' platform. Mendelsohn requested and was granted the opportunity to address the Assembly. He began by reviewing the events leading to that moment:

> The spirit of Cleveland has been diminished. In the intervening months the priorities voted the Black agenda have been watered down. Yesterday, the Black Caucus, through Mr. Henry, tried to get this major issue re-established, and was defeated, and again this morning, rejected. Our Black delegates of BAC have now left the room. They have left this Assembly, and they have left our movement, because life and time are short and running out very swiftly, and because the Assembly is returning to business as usual and to the position of Black people at the back of the bus.[14]

Mendelsohn's *j'accuse* struck a nerve. A howl of anguish and rage erupted from the Assembly. There was scarcely an opportunity to continue, but he did. Announcing his personal grief at the Assembly's decision, he concluded with his personal decision to leave the Assembly, and he invited others who shared his feelings to join him at the Arlington Street Church, one block away.

The next minutes saw the beginning of an event which would live in denominational lore, known simply as "the walkout." There had been no prearrangement. It was totally spontaneous. The delegates who filed out of the Assembly with Mendelsohn were expressing their utter frustration and despair with the course of Assembly events and the character of the denomination that was reflected in those events.

Of the 400-plus Unitarian Universalist delegates and visitors who filed into the Arlington Street Church, a few may have perceived the walkout as an act of liberation echoed in the words of FULLBAC co-chair

David Parke: "We are liberated from the intransigent racists of the Assembly."[15] Most were possessed of no such certainty. All participants in the walkout were white: All recognized that a symbolic step affirming solidarity with black leadership had been taken.

Those who remained in the Assembly were filled with consternation. The most poignant words spoken came from UUA President Dana Greeley. This was Greeley's final Assembly as president of the Unitarian Universalist Association. He had intended a much different closure of his presidential term, and the walkout left him dumbfounded:

> It was almost too much for me. . . . Here was my minister [Greeley remained a member of Arlington Street Church during his terms as president], walking out on my administration and my Board and my Assembly (and his) and going over to my church (and his) for a rump session or to form a dissident or splinter group. And it was the church under whose roof the American Unitarian Association had been organized, and which had been supportive of the AUA in all its vicissitudes for over 140 years.[16]

A photograph in the issue of the UU Laymen's League journal *Respond* devoted to the Assembly captures a moment of contact between Greeley and Mendelsohn. Each is smiling, but the atmosphere of the photo is heavy with tension. Mendelsohn is reaching out, his forearm on Greeley's shoulder, his hand embracing Greeley's neck. Mendelsohn might be saying, "I must do what I must do, but I will not let you go until you understand, even if you cannot bless this action."

Certainly Greeley never blessed "the walkout," nor did he fully understand the reasons for it. It would remain an unresolved concern years after the fact, affecting his relationship to Mendelsohn. Even though Mendelsohn had managed Greeley's campaign for re-election to the UUA presidency in 1965, Mendelsohn would not receive Greeley's endorsement when he made his own bid for the presidency in 1977. The depths of feeling dividing the two denominational leaders accurately reflected the deep divisions that "the walkout" (and indeed the issue that caused it) occasioned within Unitarian Universalism.

Another photograph, this one from the cover of *Respond*, captures the spirit of the gathering at the Arlington Street Church that was to call itself "the Moral Caucus." The photo is of the Arlington Street Church chancel. A blond and bearded youth relaxes shirtless against the chancel rail; on the stairs leading to the high pulpit a young woman waits her turn to take the pulpit microphone, which is occupied by UUA presidential candidate and BUUC supporter the Rev. Aron Gilmartin. The photo captures the spirit of participatory democracy that permeated the church.

Participatory it was, organized it was not. The walkout was an act of conscience on the part of each individual who joined it. As Aron Gilmartin, speaking for the Moral Caucus to the Assembly on the following day, pointed out, each walkout participant had acted without consultation or prior agreement. Although they had acted independently, their actions had brought them into new fellowship with each other; they could, in Gilmartin's estimation, be an emerging organization. Eventually an organization, the Fellowship for Renewal, did develop out of the Moral Caucus.

Several of the speakers at the Arlington Street Church had urged organization. "I'm an organizer, not an anarchist," declared the Rev. Stephen Fritchman. "Organize—no matter what else turns out."[17] And Richard Nash, a former member of the Unitarian Universalist Commission on Religion and Race, told the church gathering, "If we will have any influence, if we will be able to use what power we gathered here, we will have to organize."[18]

Meanwhile, the Assembly had immediately dispatched a delegation that met separately with representatives of FULLBAC and BUUC. The delegation urged both groups, and those who had aligned themselves with them in the Moral Caucus, to return to the Assembly, but without making promises of any kind to either group.[19] On the following morning, members of the Moral Caucus responded to this invitation. But when they filed back into the General Assembly, delegate badges turned upside down as an identifying mark, the calls for organization had been largely ignored.

The uncertainties of their separated situation weighed heavily upon them. They had taken a risk by leaving the Assembly voluntarily. It was possible that they would not be welcomed back if they refused the invitations extended by the denominational leadership. They knew that their leaving and their continued absence had created a gaping hole in the Assembly fabric that was felt deeply by those who remained. The Assembly wanted them to return. But for how long would the Assembly be so cordial in extending an invitation to the dissidents? No one at either the Assembly or the Arlington Street Church knew the answer.

The Moral Caucus was aware that its power rested upon its existence as a unified group—not just a random gathering of individuals, but persons assembled together in a common purpose. Its members believed that this power would be sufficient to encourage the General Assembly to deal with the issues that had occasioned the walkout in the first place. But this belief was not well founded. The Assembly's immediate move to dispatch a delegation to invite the Caucus to return suggests that the Assembly's concern did not extend to a willingness to make substantive changes or address the issues that lay behind the walkout. In addition, the swift appearance of the Assembly's delegation at Arlington Street Church indicated that the Assembly viewed the walkout as a result of heated emotions, rather than deep intellectual and moral conviction.

Thus, the Moral Caucus returned to an Assembly that was essentially unchanged from the day before. But they returned in the belief that their continued presence would make a difference. Richard Nash has speculated that "if the Black Caucus could have counted on the Moral Caucus to be organized, to maintain its numbers and to stay out for a strategic length of time, its decision about when to return would have been different, and could have been more productive."[20] While I do not dispute the cogency of this observation, I believe it does not take into consideration the substantial pressure being exerted upon the embryonic Moral Caucus. In addition, it tends to minimize the substantial accomplishments of the walkout and the Moral Caucus's formation.

In fact, the walkout had accomplished something of paramount significance: It demonstrated to BUUC that the promises and commitments made at Selma, Alabama in 1965, at the Emergency Conference on The Black Rebellion in 1967, and at the Cleveland General Assembly in 1968 would not be totally ignored. Because of this, the walkout succeeded in keeping BUUC in the denomination, and the denomination itself in the forefront of religious organizations' efforts towards black empowerment. The walkout was a dramatic demonstration of solidarity with black Unitarian Universalists.

The failure of the walkout and the resulting Moral Caucus to accomplish more can be attributed to the nature and the dynamics of the occasion. Groups of people mobilized by a particular external event or circumstance calling them to action are inevitably vastly different in direction and accomplishment from groups organized with structured inner direction and discipline. By its very nature, the externally mobilized group cannot be depended upon for cooperation on common objectives— cooperation that was evident in such organized groups as BUUC and FULLBAC.

But, spontaneously and single-handedly, the Rev. Jack Mendelsohn had effectively mobilized the walkout. The pressures of the occasion militated against the kind of organization (e.g., protracted discussion of the reasons for the walkout) that would insure complete understanding and agreement among all persons involved. There was no opportunity to develop a platform of action to be brought back to the Assembly.

For its part, the Assembly had no opportunity to move from surprise, shock, anger, sympathy, and other emotional reactions triggered by the event to a deeper understanding of the issues that had occasioned it in the first place. Because of these confusions, the walkout would long remain an unhealed wound in the denomination's consciousness. And the pain it occasioned would obscure the accomplishments which it achieved.

Following the return of the Moral Caucus to the Assembly, Kelton Sams of Houston, Texas, the vice-chairperson of BUUC, refocused the issue before the Assembly, saying, "We are not here to make a show. I move funding of BAWA or BAC—but not both!"[21] The motion, forcing the choice between BAC and BAWA, was adopted by a vote of 798 to 737 —a difference of only 61 votes, indicating the division, uncertainty, and confusion that prevailed in the Assembly.[22] The next vote was taken on which agency would be funded. The result was a foregone conclusion: BAC was funded for another year.

For six months following the General Assembly in Boston, the Unitarian Universalist Association Administration (led by a newly elected president, the Rev. Robert West) and the UUA Board of Trustees struggled with the General Assembly mandate to fully fund BAC for another year. It also struggled with a budget deficit. The two votes at the General Assemblies in 1968 and 1969 indicated that Unitarian Universalists wished the black agenda to have top priority and meant to commit themselves to that priority with dependable financial support, but the Board seriously questioned whether or not the denominational budget could sustain the level of support that the General Assemblies had voted.

On January 24, 1970, the UUA Board of Trustees voted not to reverse an earlier decision it had made to cut the voted allocation to the Black Affairs Council by $50,000.[23] Ostensibly, the cut in allocated funds would help the UUA spread the one-million-dollar commitment to BAC over a five-year rather than the four-year period which had been originally agreed upon. But this decision marked the beginning of the end of the intense and dramatic black empowerment controversy within the UUA.

When they learned of the Board's decision, BAC found itself in a "Catch-22" situation. As a "funded affiliate" of the UUA, it could not raise funds for itself, and yet the funds which had been voted to it were being cut. BAC members perceived this funding cut as the final affront meted out to it by the UUA Board of Trustees. In its statement of disaffiliation from the Unitarian Universalist Association, BAC declared:

> The Board's response to BAC has been comparable to the response that white institutions normally give to Black Americans—racist and reactionary. In the struggle being waged by Black Unitarian Universalists to find new ways for predominantly white institutions to relate to the Black American community we find this conflict between the Board and the People most interesting. . . . We feel that the majority of white Unitarian Universalists want to see the BAC program continue. BAC is the most viable program the denomination has, and its imaginative structure and style make it a model that other denominations have

already begun to follow for relating to the Black American community. Therefore, we now appeal to all who recognize the necessity for the program's continuance and growth to back our efforts by funneling financial support directly to the Black Affairs Council.[24]

The decision to disaffiliate from the UUA brought to an end a significant chapter in the denomination's history of race relations. After disaffiliation BAC would remain a Unitarian Universalist program, but it would no longer be a program of the Unitarian Universalist Association. Thus it would be able to solicit program funds from individual Unitarian Universalists and member churches and fellowships.

A former member of the Black Unitarian Universalist Caucus offered the following harsh but apt judgment: "We were the first denomination to act on behalf of black empowerment; we were the first denomination to turn our backs on black empowerment."[25]

Notes

1. Mark Green, *Commonwealth,* June 3, 1969, p. 211.
2. Minutes of the UUA Board of Trustees, June 22, 1968.
3. *Ibid.*
4. Daniel G. Higgins, Jr., "The UUA Color Line Controversy (1967–1969): Theological Implications," paper presented at Collegium, Craigville, MA, October 1979, p. 13.
5. FULLBAC Subcommittee on the Statler Hotel (Joan Garnish, Chair), "Hilton Hotel Inquiry" (Fact paper), March 1969, p. 1.
6. *Ibid.*
7. Jeremy Taylor, "What the Fight Was All About," *Respond,* Vol. 4, No. 1, September 1969, p. 3.
8. Jack Mendelsohn, sermon, Arlington Street Church, Boston, July 1969.
9. Mary Lou Thompson, "The 1969 General Assembly," *The Bridge* (Unitarian Universalist Women's Federation), September 1969, p. 7.
10. Stephen H. Fritchman, *Heretic* (Boston: Beacon Press, 1977), p. 321.
11. *Ibid.,* p. 322.
12. Homer A. Jack, "Like It Was," *Respond,* Vol. 4, No. 1, September 1969.
13. Thompson, "The 1969 General Assembly," p. 8.
14. Fritchman, *Heretic,* p. 323.
15. Thompson, "The 1969 General Assembly," p. 8.

16. Dana Greeley, 25 *Beacon Street and Other Recollections* (Boston: Skinner House, 1971), p. 126.
17. Fritchman, *Heretic*, p. 325.
18. Richard Nash, 'What Happened in Boston" (mimeograph, 1969), p. 3.
19. Jack, "Like It Was."
20. Nash, "What Happened in Boston," p. 4.
21. Thompson, "The 1969 General Assembly," p. 9.
22. *1970 Directory* (Boston: Unitarian Universalist Association, 1970), p. 175.
23. Minutes of the UUA Board of Trustees, January 24, 1970.
24. Raymond C. Hopkins, memorandum to UUA Board of Trustees, March 30, 1970.
25. Henry Hampton, personal communication, October 4, 1982.

Illustrations

Images from the 1969 General Assembly

Harold Wilson, Ben Scott, and Richard Traylor, members of the Black Affairs Council, at a seminar. *Photo: Mitch Turner.*

The Rev. Dwight Brown (Dallas, Texas) and Dr. Donald S. Harrington (New York City).

Hayward Henry and others. *Photo: Dan Bernstein.*

Jack Mendelsohn and Dana Greeley.

A white youth and two black BAC supporters lock hands over a commandeered microphone. *Photo: Steven Hansen.*

Hayward Henry and the Rev. Stephen Fritchman.

Robert West at the GA podium, with Dana Greeley looking on.
Photo: Donald Wright Patterson, Jr.

Wayne Arneson and others at Arlington Street Church during the walkout.

Harold Wilson (with cigarette), the Rev. Aron Gilmartin (standing at right), Hayward Henry (seated at right), and others.

Chapter 4

BAC Bonds and the Black Humanist Fellowship

In January 1970 the UUA Board of Trustees moved to white out black empowerment. The Board, primarily but not exclusively white, and operating under the pressure of a newly discovered major financial short-fall, voted to cut $50,000 from the $250,000 budgeted allocation for the Black Affairs Council (BAC). This action was the first in a series that would significantly compromise Unitarian Universalism's attempts to address the issue of race for the next quarter of a century.

Four months later the UUA Board took another, more extreme step. On the recommendation of UUA President Robert West and the UUA Finance Committee, it voted to terminate *all* funding for BAC. BAC and its white supporters bitterly protested the action, calling it racist in so far as it "will function to the further disadvantage of black people to the further advantage of white people."[1]

Was this decision racist? The UUA Board did retain the money that would have gone to BAC to be placed against the denomination's fiscal shortfall. Since the denomination was (and is) overwhelmingly white, whites stood to gain from such a decision; since BAC represented black initiatives addressing the need for black empowerment, blacks (inside and outside the denomination) stood to lose from the decision.

However, the charge of racism deserves further examination. The decision was not motivated by intentionally intolerant feelings, nor did it come from a posture of "color-blindness," promoting spurious claims that color is irrelevant. The board members recognized the importance of race but chose to ignore it when considered against the denomination's financial difficulty. Fiscal solvency trumped social vision. Since the board did not take the issue back to the churches (a move that would have been difficult, seeing that it had already ignored the vote of two General Assemblies in reducing the BAC allocation in the first place) or engage in alternative strategies for raising the money, the charge of institutional racism appears inescapable.

BAC, for its part, recognized what was happening and chose to change its relationship with the UUA from "affiliate" (funded directly from the UUA annual budget) to "associate" (the status held by the UU Service Committee). This move would allow BAC to retain its UU affiliation while giving it direct access to individual UU congregations for fundraising and support. The move was agreeable to the UUA administration. It would relieve the UUA of having to honor its institutional commitment to BAC and nullify the debate regarding the fairness of funding BAWA, the group advocating an alternative approach to race empowerment.

While it is easy to understand why the UUA would welcome BAC's move to disaffiliate from the UUA, it is hard to understand BAC's motivation. Was BAC operating on the assumption that the individual UU congregations, many with long histories of unwillingness to pay their fair share of money for denominational support and with few black members, would be more amenable to financing black empowerment? Or was BAC simply expressing its resignation and despair at the UUA Board's intransigence?

One possible explanation of both the UUA's and BAC's positions at this juncture comes from scholars of whiteness and racial attitudes in multi-cultural societies, who suggest that racism is so pervasive in black-white relations in the U.S. that its effects are similar to those of terrorism. African Americans must constantly mobilize resources of body and mind to defend themselves against "micro-aggressions" by whites. These micro-aggressions are so routine and habitual that the white person committing them is typically unconscious of how the black person perceives them.² As a result the white person, unaware of her or his racist affront, is baffled and confused by the angry reaction the act elicits from the black person.

While such an explanation may help to lighten the painful weight of racism itself, it does nothing to mitigate the UUA's self-serving explanations of BAC's move from affiliate to associate status. The UUA claimed that BAC (1) was reacting angrily to the initial cut of $50,000 from its allocation and (2) believed that it could raise more money by dealing directly with UU congregations. Both explanations are not only false but also disingenuous. BAC was indeed angry, but its anger, viewed in the context of its rocky relationship with the UUA, was neither impetuous nor excessive. And its move toward independent fund raising was, at least in part, an expression of its disappointment at the UUA's lack of commitment to racial justice.

The UUA was also oblivious that BAC had been working with a black constituency beyond Unitarian Universalism to establish empowered black enterprises. BAC had made grants to a variety of black social organizations, which thus looked to it (and, by extension, to Unitarian Universalism) as a vehicle of black liberation. The UUA's partial funding cut placed BAC in a double bind: it had to reassure its black constituency that the Unitarian Universalists were sincere in their efforts to fund black empowerment while, at the same time, expressing anger not only at having funds cut but also at the UUA Board's knowingly violating the will of the General Assembly.

Now, as a new General Assembly approached, BAC believed that the UUA would use its move from affiliate to associate status as a rationale for refusing to honor the original four-year, one-million-dollar commitment to BAC that had been voted at the General Assembly in 1968 and re-affirmed in 1969.

While some members of both BUUC and BAC attended the 1970 General Assembly in Seattle, Washington, there was no formal BAC presence. BAC had argued that its change in status did not release the denomination from honoring the moral commitment that two General Assemblies had made, but it received little support at the 1970 General Assembly. Convened in the relatively tranquil far Northwest and free of the racial tensions which had marked two previous General Assemblies, the Seattle GA voted for fiscal stability as the prime denominational priority. But years later, Rose Edington would ask in her D.Min. dissertation, "Priority for whom?"[3]

While the Seattle General Assembly marked the end of one chapter of the Empowerment Controversy, that Assembly was not without its curious aspects. While overwhelmingly rejecting BAC's request that the original commitment to black empowerment be honored, the Assembly also passed a resolution advocating the funding of BAWA by individual congregations as "an inspirational exhortation for UU churches and fellowship to undertake the burden (of funding) rather than a denominational commitment of dollars."[4]

As BAC's struggle for financial support from the UUA was faltering, BAC was also gathering its strength for a second initiative, a bolder move in support of black empowerment. Even before the formation of BUUC in 1967, Benjamin Scott, a black Unitarian Universalist, research chemist, and leader of the Boston black community, was developing the concept of local development bonds, a concept that would reach beyond black community organizing and generate broader support for local empowerment programs. Scott and BAC created "BAC bonds," instruments of financial investment that would be sold to churches, fellowships, and individual Unitarian Universalists as a means of bringing dollars for economic development into black communities. This would be "venture capital," funds invested not only with the expectation of making a profit but also with the wider goal of advancing black communities and challenging the rigid financial institutions which, in the words of BAC secretary Richard Traylor, "supported the status quo and made violent racial conflict more likely." Traylor hoped the bonds would generate "new economic development in black communities, featuring white aid without white control."[5]

The proceeds from the sale of BAC bonds would be used to make loans to and investments in black-controlled enterprises. The criteria for making such investments would be a high probability of success and adequate financial return on the initial investment. To these traditional criteria was added a third, evidence of potential social utility in alleviating powerlessness and the dependent status of black communities.[6]

70

Who would be empowered to make such judgments? Even at the outset BAC could boast an impressive roster of names (several drawn from university economics faculties and law firms in the Washington, DC area). As Traylor stated, however, "These businessmen and financiers who would be conducting the evaluations would undergo special orientation created for improving their level of social sensitivity. As a result the program will have the advantage of high input of expertise, but all decisions relative to investment will be made by the black-controlled BAC Investment Corporation."[7]

Traylor's enthusiasm was justified. A year earlier, even as the UUA Board of Trustees was reducing its commitment to black empowerment, BAC could announce that $200,000 had already been pledged: $50,000 from the Liberal Religious Youth organization, the first denominational institutional subscription; $25,000 from the UU Women's Federation; and $125,000 from the First Unitarian Society of West Newton, Massachusetts.

For the second time in three years the Unitarian Universalists had acted prophetically. In 1968 the denomination at its General Assembly had voted almost a quarter of its institutional budget to fund black empowerment before any other religious institution in the U.S. made such a commitment. Now, in 1970, BAC had created an investment corporation and an investment instrument to address the black community's need not only for aid but also for capital. By any standard this was a remarkable witness to the worth and the dignity of human beings everywhere.

The very idea of capital investment bonds brought BAC into contact with many agencies well beyond the borders of Unitarian Universalism. Such an undertaking demanded the sanction of the U.S. Securities and Exchange Commission (SEC) and, of course, the Internal Revenue Service (IRS). Having received federal approval, the new Black Capital Investment Corporation needed to position itself to receive funds not only from UU churches and individuals, but also from the Federal Government as well. A major undertaking was in the works.

In order to receive federal funds, Benjamin Scott helped the Black Capital Investment Corporation to register as a Minority Enterprise Small Business Investment Corporation (MESBIC). The new MESBIC status,

71

however, also meant that more than one member of BAC was empowered to control the funds received, so that multiple people could make conflicting decisions. That fact would have very serious consequences for BAC's future.

While the promise of federal funds was enticing, and while individuals could and did purchase bonds, BAC believed the primary market for its bonds was UU churches and fellowships. Unfortunately the UU congregations, reflecting the spirit of retrenchment and withdrawal exhibited by the UUA administration's retreat from its commitment to BAC, proved unreceptive to the opportunity presented by the bonds. Why?

While marketing BAC bonds to individual congregations may have initially seemed like the solution to the dilemma posed by the UUA's withdrawal of funds, once again this was a case of economics contradicting the principles of faith. According to the Rev. John Hickey, the senior minister and executive director of the Unitarian Universalist Urban Ministry and a former executive and attorney with IBM, confusion resulted from BAC's attempt to combine charitable good works with the capitalist free market. From a "good works" perspective, BAC bonds represented a disciplined way of investing in stable, locally-owned community enterprises. As an investment, however, BAC bonds represented a very high risk, with the prospect of very little, if any, financial return.

This is not to suggest that BAC bonds were in any way misrepresented. To the contrary, BAC was very direct and realistic about the high-risk elements of its proposal. The group did meet all of the regulatory and market requirements for issuing the bonds, but the offering documents made clear that the social objective was primary. The proposed investments were speculative ventures that could not obtain financing elsewhere. The potential investor was warned of the "substantial economic risk" of losing both interest and principal. There were no predictions that, if successful, the bonds would pay an above-average return. If judged on the basis of market criteria alone, the investment formula simply did not "close."

Even so, if the UU congregations to which BAC bonds were marketed had had sufficient funds in their budgets for social justice, the formula might have worked. The vast majority of those congregations did not.

Funds allocated for social justice and community outreach purposes generally were then, and still remain, a small fraction of UU church budgets.

Many UU congregations do have endowments, money amassed over time and separated from day-to-day budgetary needs, to be used for extraordinary needs or opportunities. Members of BAC and FULLBAC suggested that churches should consider investing their endowment funds in BAC bonds. Given the all-but-sacred status that most churches attach to their endowment funds, however, it is not surprising that few were prepared to take such a risk. In addition, endowment funds are often governed by fiduciary obligations established by state law and set forth in congregational bylaws, which impose "prudent investor" standards. These obligations and standards would likely give pause to any endowment committee considering investing in BAC bonds. The churches that did invest in the bonds did so primarily as statements of faith rather than as investments for financial gain.

Three congregations, however, did respond: the First Unitarian Society of West Newton, Massachusetts; the First Unitarian Congregational Society of Brooklyn, New York; and All Souls Church, Washington, DC. Following West Newton's lead, Brooklyn pledged $150,000 to the bonds and All Souls pledged $250,000. While individuals pledged additional, smaller amounts, the total never exceeded $800,000.

The West Newton church was the first individual congregation to make a commitment to BAC bonds. Prompted by the vigorous urging of its new minister, the Rev. Clyde Dodder—a white man new to Unitarian Universalism, who had originally been attracted to the denomination by its history of social activism and social involvement—this essentially white, suburban Boston congregation voted to invest $125,000 in BAC bonds. The Society's investment committee recommended that the money be drawn partially from the church's endowment and partially from a capital fund drive. When brought to the congregation for approval, the proposal passed by a vote of 55 in favor and 49 opposed. The narrow vote fueled a furious and protracted debate that lasted for 13 months. At one point a former minister threatened to sue the church for dereliction of its fiduciary responsibilities, and the church treasurer refused to sign a check earmarked for BAC bond purchase. The struggle proved too much for the Rev. Dodder, who resigned his position as Newton's minister and later withdrew from Unitarian Universalist ministerial fellowship.

All Souls Church of Washington, DC boasted one of the two largest black constituencies within Unitarian Universalism. It had a strong record of social and political involvement in the affairs of both the city and the nation. Its former assistant minister James Reeb had been martyred during the civil rights struggle in Selma, Alabama. At the urging of its previous senior minister, the Rev. Duncan Howlett, the congregation had called an outstanding black leader, the Rev. David Eaton, to its pulpit. The congregation of All Souls was itself deeply engaged in a local project of urban renewal, the rehabilitation of a section of Washington bordering its property. When it voted to buy $250,000 in BAC bonds, it did so with the understanding that the money would be directed toward the project with which the church was already engaged. Eventually the money became part of the litigation that would embroil BAC in the 1970s, but All Souls continued its commitment to the urban renewal project. The Rev. Easton's leadership from the very beginnings of his All Souls ministry and continuing throughout this stressful period was masterful, providing BUUC/BAC with enormous personal and institutional support and encouragement.

The third congregation to invest over $100,000 in BAC bonds had no local project to which it might direct its contribution. However, the First Unitarian Society of Brooklyn, New York did have a strong tradition of social involvement ranging from financial assistance to the Unitarian movements in India and Transylvania to support for local expressions of empowerment such as the Settlement House movement. One such house, the Fulton Street Center, was a key element in the Brooklyn congregation's "awareness training," as church member James Gunning put it. Involvement with the Center sensitized the congregation to the lives and problems of the black and white underclass around them,. To those so prepared, the so-called "black rebellion" came as no surprise. Brooklyn sent the largest individual church delegation to the historic Biltmore Conference in 1967, at which BUUC was formed.

Brooklyn's senior minister, the Rev. Donald McKinney, had been preaching black empowerment since the early 1960s. His involvement had even led to a personal meeting with Malcolm X four years before his assassination. When the call came to invest in BAC bonds, McKinney and the Brooklyn congregation were ready. Years later McKinney would reflect, "It was a demanding time, and costly, but we did survive and in certain fundamental ways we were made stronger—even in failure—because we were able to respond when persuaded that time, circumstance and our commitment as a community of faith demanded firm institutional response, while still being respectful of the difference among us."[8]

Interestingly, in addition to recognition by BUUC/BAC for its support, Brooklyn received a special award from BAWA for having provided more opportunities to hear the BAWA position than any other Unitarian Universalist congregation within the UUA.

***

A photo hangs in the Dana Greeley room at UUA headquarters—vintage 1968, the Greeley administration. White men sitting and standing, white women seated on the floor at their feet next to Peter Putnam's seeing-eye dog. Located at the far end of the group photo is one black face: Henry Hampton, the lone African American working in the UUA publicity department and the only UUA staff person to be a member of BUUC. Hampton would later leave the UUA to create the documentary film organization Blackside and produce the acclaimed *Eyes on the Prize* series. But in 1968 Hampton's job was to communicate important developments within UUism.

In April 1968, the *Boston Globe* published an article by Henry Hampton entitled, "Will the New Black Church Split the White Establishment?" Better than any of the whites at UUA headquarters including President Greeley, Hampton saw a split coming between white and black UUs. The force behind the so-called "New Black Church" was black humanism, which did not ultimately split the white establishment but did drive a wedge into BUUC that would eventually result in a split into two BACs and the final dissolution of the black empowerment movement within Unitarian Universalism.

In April 1968 Martin Luther King, Jr. had been assassinated. It was a moment when black Unitarian Universalists shared their pain and rage with their non-UU brothers and sisters. However, the profound distress affecting the black community generally was, within UU circles, somewhat mitigated by the belief that a new black religious perspective was emerging, one that would transcend the UU circumstances of its origin to occasion a spiritual renewal for black people everywhere. The name of this spiritual initiative was black humanism. According to Benjamin Scott, "black humanism recognizes that the ethic and relationship of human beings is the greater law . . . that human beings should interact with each other and that their needs (emotional, psychic and physical) should become the prime spiritual motivating force."[9]

According to a 1969 article by one of its promoters, the Rev. Mwalimu Imara (then minister of the Arlington St. Church in Boston), black humanism was based on four principles: collectivism, naturalism, spiritualism, and humanism, each with a particular philosophical grounding. Its central claim was that "all black persons are legitimate members of the oppressed community," and therefore its object was "group salvation as opposed to individual salvation; there is no individualism outside of the whole of black people."[10]

Black humanism's agenda was never in doubt. In his articulation of black humanism's spiritual system, Imara affirmed "the transforming human process beginning with birth and ending with nationhood." Black humanism, according to Imara, "places less value on the individual transcendence and memorializes in history the transcendence of the group, the community of the nation."[11]

Imara, a duly ordained and fellowshipped UU minister, made no mention of his ties to Unitarian Universalism in this article. Although his exegesis of black humanism was published in the BUUC/BAC newsletter, Imara explicitly separated the goals of black humanism from those of BUUC, whose primary energies were addressed to challenging the UU movement. "A Black Humanist Fellowship," he wrote, "is a spiritual institution which articulated and developed an ideology, an ethic, a vision; new perspectives about institutions; new theoretical constructs; programs, projects, ministries and movements."[12]

Imara was not alone in his perception of a wider context for black humanism. BAC chairperson Hayward Henry had spoken of "new black religious forms" in 1969,[13] and UU layperson Alex Poinsett reflected the wider perspective of black humanism in an *Ebony* magazine article entitled "It's Nation Time."[14] According to Poinsett, the leadership of BAC (including chairperson Hayward Henry and executive secretary Richard Traylor) was seeking to create a close alliance with larger black liberation movements, especially the Congress of African People, of which Henry had become the national chairman. The Poinsett article focused on an international gathering of the Congress that attracted 2,700 delegates, including 350 from 35 African and Third World countries.[15] In addition, the Congress was one of the programs funded by BAC in 1970–1971.

Some Black UU Caucus members were questioning the closer relationship that was developing between the Congress of African People and the leadership of BAC. Specific concerns included that Hayward Henry's chairing both organizations constituted a conflict of interest; that BUUC staff members did not have the authority to invest either time or BAC resources in the Congress; and that the Congress's separatist ideology was not consistent with the ideology of BUUC, which struggled to retain its relationship with Unitarian Universalism at a time when most members of BUUC were not personally active in UU congregations.

A fundamental point of contention was the proposal to change the name of the Black Unitarian Universalist Caucus to the Black Humanist Fellowship, thereby symbolically dropping the association with the UUA, its denominational "home." By November 1972, a breakaway Fellowship had formed within BUUC, and a subcommittee was appointed to develop a proposal for the name change. The rationale was that the change would facilitate greater involvement with the larger black liberation movements, especially the Congress of African People. In addition, it was argued that the name change would effect a divorce from the "indifferent UUA," which would serve to re-inspire the BUUC constituency.

The timing of the proposed name change is curious. It came only months after the UUA, which had in effect washed its hands of black empowerment in Seattle in 1970, had courted BAC's return to a place in the UUA annual budget and voted it an associate member once again in

March 1972. The ostensible reason for the West administration's change of heart was a grant to the UUA from the North Shore Unitarian Society of Plandome, New York (now known as the UU Congregation at Shelter Rock) of $250,000, 72% of which was earmarked for BAC. BAC accepted the renewed status of associate membership and the funding, which, in the opinion of BAC member Hilda Mason, "helped to heal some of the wounds."[16]

In light of the Plandome grant, the charge of "indifference" by the UUA as a reason for changing BUUC's name lost resonance. If BUUC changed its name, the grant and BAC's tax-exempt status would be lost, and the BAC bond program would be placed in jeopardy. For these reasons, BAC treasurer Benjamin Scott and a few other BAC board members vigorously opposed the name change.

Just before BUUC's sixth annual meeting, in 1973, BAC vice-chair Gwen Thomas attempted to head off the Black Humanist Fellowship move for separation from Unitarian Universalism. She urged that the Fellowship be supported as "a program adjunct rather than change the BUUC constitution itself," which a formal change of name would require.[17] The move failed.

The sixth annual meeting of BUUC was both the most decisive and the most contentious gathering in the organization's history. Ever since the UUA General Assembly in Seattle in 1970, local caucuses had expressed degrees of dissatisfaction with BUUC. The Chicago Caucus had reservations about BAC bonds; the Los Angeles Caucus had a dispute with national chairperson Hayward Henry. At the fourth annual meeting there had been a call for decentralization. At that meeting Henry had declined to be a candidate for chairperson of BUUC, and the Rev. Harold Wilson was elected. By the time of the sixth meeting, dissatisfaction had flamed into open conflict over the suggested name change to the Black Humanist Fellowship.

There is no record of the proceedings of the meeting. Charges and countercharges are rife: an arbitrary decision was made to raise the meeting registration fees; there were no provisions for observers; guards were posted at entrances, and those allowed access to the assembly were screened. A challenge to the legality of the meeting by some BUUC/BAC members was overruled, and the dissidents (including Gwendolyn Thomas, Dalmas Taylor, Louth Gotherard and Benjamin Scott) left the meeting to gather separately, calling themselves "the Political Committee of BUUC."

The meeting's only business was the vote to change the constitutional name of the organization from Black UU Caucus to Black Humanist Fellowship and the election of a new slate of officers. The name change passed; it was a fateful decision.

The first outcome was a lawsuit organized by Dalmas Taylor and Benjamin Scott to stop the name change from taking effect. Taylor, a member of both BUUC and the UUA Board of Trustees, wrote that the decision to change the BUUC constitution was an attempt by the Black Humanist Fellowship to organize itself into another denomination, which would end the relationship of BUUC with the churches of the UUA, violate the assumptions among UU churches that BUUC was a UU agency for support and development in the black community, and jeopardize the contributions of nearly one million dollars in BAC bonds for that purpose.

The court's decision, however, did not rest on any of these factors. According to the court, the issue turned on whether the BUUC annual meeting had a quorum. Because they had not closely adhered to the quorum definition in their own bylaws at previous annual meetings, the court ruled in favor of the Black Humanist Fellowship defendants, chairperson Harold Wilson and secretary Richard Traylor.

The judgment stunned the plaintiffs. They immediately appealed the judge's decision. However, the verdict had already placed the future of BAC bonds in economic limbo. With questions about their legal viability and the destination of the money in doubt, contributions dried up.

The confusion was not limited to the future of BAC bonds. The entire structure of UU initiatives for black empowerment was in disarray. Because of the legal standoff, BAC's assets and investments were frozen. The situation was so absurd that there were now two Black Affairs Councils, the one that had been in office before the contested annual meeting, and another elected at the meeting. It would be another three years before the legal dispute reached any conclusion.

Because money played such an important role, it is easy to conclude that the Empowerment Controversy was about money. But in fact, the struggle that embroiled Unitarian Universalists in the late '60s and early '70s was, in the words of current UUA financial advisor Larry Ladd, "not about money but about us."[18]

In the 1998 afterword to his exploratory study of black liberation theology *Is God a White Racist?*, UU theologian William Jones asserts that the period of black theology's emergence (and the eruption of the Empowerment Controversy on the UU scene) was a time of exploration without agreed-upon intellectual maps or charts. Says Jones: "Its own practitioners were still unclear about what [black theology] entailed for theologizing and even less clear about how to translate its theory into concrete strategies for economic, social and political reconstruction."[19]

The same assessment could be made of the Black Affairs Council. Some BAC leaders advocated an economic agenda of black capitalism, the development of black investment opportunities, and the creation of mortgage companies to finance affordable housing in mixed-income neighborhoods. Others embraced an Africanist agenda of cooperative economics and an emphasis on the extended family derived from the Swahili concept of *ujima*. This far more radical alternative, embraced by the leaders of what became the Black Humanist Fellowship, would lead its proponents away from Unitarian Universalism.

In retrospect, the seeds of this radical departure from mainline UUism were sown almost from the beginning of the Empowerment Controversy. The denomination had been so focused on the deep differences between integrationist philosophy (represented by BAWA) and liberationist philosophy (BAC) that even some of those closely connected with BAC could not fully appreciate the new directions in which BAC was moving.

In addition, there had been long-standing spiritual and theological divisions between many black and white UUs. Long before the Empowerment Controversy broke upon UU consciousness, African Americans had voiced their concerns about the failure of UU theology and liturgy to speak to their condition. Worship services in UU churches, societies and fellowships were considered excessively verbal and cerebral,

lacking the spirit-moving music and exuberant preaching that characterized black religious celebrations. UU worship was white worship, which
belied the "all welcome" signs gracing most UU sanctuary doors.

In addition to the general feeling that black spiritual needs were not
being met by UU worship practices, African Americans were increasingly
aware that their presence in UU congregations served essentially to salve
the consciences of the whites rather than to advance the concerns of
black liberation. Ultimately some began to argue that the presence of
blacks in UU congregations was, in fact, counterproductive to black liberation, since it served to reassure whites that African Americans neither
needed nor desired liberation.

This perception efforts was given powerful expression at the 1971
General Assembly in Washington, DC in a worship service sponsored by
the Black Humanist Fellowship. The preacher, the Rev. Mwalimu Imara
(then minister at the Arlington St. Church in Boston and a member of the
BHF), likened the position of blacks in UU churches to that of a Jewish
woman whose family had been gassed in Dachau Concentration Camp.
After the war the woman had re-built her life, achieved economic and
social security, and fallen in love. Her love deepened into a desire for commitment and consummation. In the course of their lovemaking the
woman was approaching climax. At that moment she caught sight of her
lover's naked shoulder, on which was a small tattoo, a mark of honor
awarded to officers at Dachau who had distinguished themselves in their
efforts to kill Jews. Rev. Imara likened the woman's pain, rage, and confusion to the condition of the African American in a UU congregation.

This anecdote captures the basic elements in the alienation of
African American Unitarian Universalists from their white co-religionists—and subsequently from each other, as expressed by the division
within the Black Affairs Council between advocates of black capitalism
and advocates of the Black Humanist Fellowship, with its Africanist social
and economic agenda.

William Jones's new afterword to *Is God a White Racist?* provides
important conceptual tools to aid in understanding what occurred among
African American UUs who were seeking liberation first through the
Black Affairs Council and subsequently through the Black Humanist

81

Fellowship. Jones speaks of how African American theologians committed to a liberation perspective, both within and outside Unitarian Universalism, were struggling to develop conceptual frameworks that expressed their unique African American understanding of liberation theology's mission and method. According to Jones, "Liberation theology's point of departure is a context where oppression is already institutionalized and legitimated." The history of the Black Unitarian Universalist Caucus is a history of struggle against UU "institutionalized and legitimated" oppression. However, as Jones points out, the task of liberation extends well beyond theology. The theory of liberation must be translated into concrete strategies for economic, social, and political reconstruction.[20] While BAC attempted to address each of these three areas (through grants to community development groups, BAC bonds, and developing ties with trans-national organizations like the Congress of African Peoples), Jones believes that BAC focused too much on economics at the expense of the social and the political realms. I believe its internal structure was insufficient to carry through such far-reaching initiatives while at the same time maintaining ties and providing reassurances to the essentially white UUA "parent body."

Notes

1. Black Affairs Council, "It Was Wrong, Save BAC," *BACground* (newsletter), 1970.
2. See, for example, Peggy McIntosh, "White Privilege and Male Privilege," in Margaret L. Andersen, ed., *Race, Class and Gender: An Anthology* (Belmont, CA: Wadsworth Publishing Co., 1992) and Ruth Brandenburg, *Displacing Whiteness* (Durham, NC: Duke University Press, 1997).
3. Rose Edington, *Crossing A Creek: Choosing Antiracism Identity as a White Woman in Unitarian Universalist Parish Ministry* (D.Min. dissertation).
4. UUA Commission on Appraisal, *Empowerment: One Denomination's Quest for Racial Justice, 1967–1982* (Boston: UUA, 1983), p. 120.
5. Richard Traylor, letter to Charles Morse, November 8, 1971.
6. *BACground*, September 1971.
7. Richard Traylor, *BACground*, September 1971.
8. Donald McKinney, sermon, First Unitarian Society of Brooklyn, May 2001.
9. UUA Commission on Appraisal, *Empowerment*, p. 24.
10. Mwalimu Imara, "Black Humanism," *BACground*, 1969.

11. *Ibid.*
12. *Ibid.*
13. UUA Commission on Appraisal, *Empowerment*, p. 48.
14. Alex Poinsett, "It's Nation Time," *Ebony*, December 1970.
15. *Ibid.*
16. UUA Commission on Appraisal, *Empowerment*, p. 47
17. Gwen Thomas, letter to BUUC Steering Committee, January 1973.
18. Larry Ladd, personal communication, May 10, 2001.
19. William Jones, *Is God A White Racist? A Preamble to Black Theology* (Boston: Beacon Press, 1998), p. 205.
20. *Ibid.*

Chapter 5

Reflections: The Undiscovered Country

In 1991, the Rev. Lisa Ward, a Unitarian Universalist minister who was then a student at Union Theological School in New York, submitted a master's thesis on "The Black Empowerment Controversy within the Unitarian Universalist Association, 1967–1970: One Religious Institution's Crisis between Intent and Routine Efficacy." Ward introduced her thesis's conclusions with the following quotation from Hamlet's "to be or not to be" soliloquy:

> . . . But that the dread of something after death,
> The undiscovered country, from whose bourn
> No traveler returns, puzzles the will,
> And makes us rather bear those ills we have
> Than fly to others that we know not of.
> Thus conscience doth make cowards of us all,
> And thus the native hue of resolution
> Is sicklied o'er with the pale cast of thought,
> And enterprises of great pitch and moment
> With this regard their current turn awry
> And lose the name of action.

Ward extends the "undiscovered country," Shakespeare's metaphor for death, to include the fear of taking action that will effect significant change. This fear is generated by an awareness that if authentic change occurs, people and social arrangements will change in ways that cannot be known or fully anticipated in advance.

In much the same manner that the nation was challenged by the Civil Rights Movement a decade earlier, the Empowerment Controversy challenged Unitarian Universalism to enter "the undiscovered country," from which we could never return to the old ways and the old dispensations. The changes that we *could* anticipate were fearsome enough, including the redistribution of power and the transformation of Unitarian Universalist associational structures. Rather than venturing into the unknown, we opted to remain in the "discovered country" of tradition and institutional preservation. In so doing, we "lost the name of action." We have yet to regain it.

The Rev. Donald McKinney, minister emeritus of the First Unitarian Congregational Society of Brooklyn, New York, says that many UUs still feel that the topic of the Empowerment Controversy should be left alone. "It is," he has said, "a painful subject, but if we are ever to hope to overcome the seemingly ever-evasive evil of racism, we must better understand its workings in the institutional life of America, and that, most assuredly, means the workings of our churches."[1]

For more than 30 years, the Empowerment Controversy, with all of its unresolved, and perhaps unresolvable, issues of race, money, and the values of liberal religion, has troubled and challenged us. The concerns that divided us then remain today. At the 2001 General Assembly in Cleveland, Ohio, site of the original vote to fund the Black Affairs Council in 1968, I led a workshop on the topic of the Controversy for ministers. Forty-five ministers attended, including several leaders of Black and White Action (BAWA) and FULLBAC, the (white) Black Affairs Council support network. While four African Americans were in attendance, none had been a member of the Black UU Caucus (BUUC) or the Black Affairs Council (BAC). One minister (white) remarked that at the time of the Controversy he was "five months short of being born."

Within this diverse group, the issues that had divided us some 30 years ago were debated with passion as intense as had been generated three decades before. The issues remain unresolved. They strike close to the very heart of liberal religion's most cherished values of freedom and

86

individualism and confront us with the still unresolved issues of race, racism, and the struggle to achieve an anti-racist perspective.

Now African Americans are beginning to gain access to Unitarian Universalist pulpits, administer significant UU institutions, provide leadership in our theological schools, and organize themselves in order to provide personal and professional support for each other in their still minimal institutional presence. These are examples of progress, but they hardly make up for the exodus of black UUs who had come into UU churches, attracted by the promise of leadership in the cause of empowerment, and left when that promise turned out to be an illusion in the wake of the events of the late 1960s and early '70s.

Perhaps we should just forget about the Empowerment Controversy, allow it to simply "burn itself out," as some have suggested. But three decades later the burning continues. The issues that the Controversy raised are too deeply embedded in our institutional life and thought. Our class biases, our notions of freedom and individualism, our attitudes about the relationship between power and love are all tested in any examination of the Empowerment Controversy.

Nor can we simply "tell the story," because there is no one story. There are stories and stories within stories. The Empowerment Controversy is a mosaic, to be assembled by many hands, black and white, knowledgeable and naïve.

A poster hangs on my office wall, given to me by a member of South Africa's Truth and Reconciliation Commission, which was established to uncover the truths of apartheid in the belief that the truth will liberate. The poster reads, "Don't let our nightmares become our children's." For some the Empowerment Controversy was a nightmare; for others it was "a dream deferred." For me it was a period that provided a searching critique of our Unitarian Universalist ethos and how it responded to a significant challenge to its established values and traditions.

The fundamental lesson of the Controversy, I believe, is a postmodern one: what we see depends on where we stand, and what we are willing to see depends on where we are willing to stand. As other observers of the Controversy have concluded, "we must train ourselves toward mutuality, the dynamic of shared power, and keep ever mindful of interdependence in our striving for self-actualization."[2] We continue to be challenged by the possibility of entering the "undiscovered country," from which, once discovered and entered, we will feel no need or desire to return to fearing difference or accepting the inequities of the status quo.

Over the past months that I have been engaged with this topic, I have listened (sometimes patiently, sometimes not) to the sentiment that the Empowerment Controversy deserves a "good leaving alone." Alternatively, some have made efforts to bypass the Controversy's still-unresolved aspects and effect a reconciliation of sorts through a kind of "forgive-and-forget" bonhomie. Such efforts at reconciliation are premature. The issues that led to the Empowerment Controversy have not been settled, nor have they been forgotten. They continue to lie beneath the surface of our institutional life, undefined and unresolved, compromising our efforts to embody our principles in subtle and not-so-subtle ways.

A case in point is the depletion of the UUA's unrestricted funds prior to the 1968 General Assembly vote to fund BAC. Although the UUA's unrestricted endowment funds had been exhausted in 1968, Dana Greeley failed to disclose this fact to the General Assembly, which voted to fund the Black Affairs Council at the rate of $250,000 a year for four years. The financial shortfall remained hidden from the denomination during the final year of the Greeley administration. Upon his election to the UUA presidency at the General Assembly in 1969, Robert West was confronted with a huge budget deficit. With the approval of the UUA Board, West set about making budgetary cuts in both program and headquarters staff in a desperate attempt to restore fiscal stability to the organization.

When the news of the UUA's financial difficulties were made public, West's administration failed to address the reason. That would have meant confronting the legacy of President Greeley and his expansionist enthusiasms, which had outdistanced the denomination's financial capabilities. West opted to forgo what would have been a painful encounter with the Greeley mystique. Instead he confronted the thankless task of bringing the denomination's budget back into balance.

Once the news of the shortfall became known, a rumor began to circulate that the denomination's fiscal problems were the result of the General Assembly votes in 1968 and 1969 to fund BAC. The West administration's failure to confront and demolish this rumor—which it could have done by making public the fact that the denomination had exhausted its unrestricted endowment funds *before* the 1968 vote to fund BAC—allowed it to circulate unchecked. Because of the UUA's "white lie," this rumor continues to circulate to this day. Such is the "ever-evasive evil of racism."[3]

In January 2001, a dozen Unitarian Universalists accepted the invitation from the Starr King School for the Ministry to come together in Berkeley, California to "get the story straight." But the "story" of the Empowerment Controversy is filled with political, social, and religious twists and turns. The goal of getting it "straight" was unrealistic. The gathering itself was challenged at the outset by several leaders of BAC and the Black Humanist Fellowship (BHF) who had declined the invitation to participate. While the dozen who did participate (six Euro-Americans and six African Americans) took the task very seriously, struggling with differing memories and interpretations of events, the results were inconclusive.

Six months after the gathering in Berkeley, Starr King published the results under the title *In Their Own Words: A Conversation with Participants in the Black Empowerment Movement within the Unitarian Universalist Association*, edited by Dr. Alicia Forsey.[4]

Of the dozen Unitarian Universalists who accepted the invitation to attend, 11 had been deeply involved and profoundly affected by the Controversy from its beginning. Each had played a vital, and voluntarily chosen, role in shaping the events, organizing the forces, and articulating the perspectives that would command the denomination's attention during its most challenging period in the second half of the 20th century. Each would share how the experience had affected him or her, how it had been life-changing and spiritually liberating. Many would remember their involvement in the Empowerment Controversy as the high point of a career and a life devoted to the principles and values of liberal religion.

I was the 12th participant in the conference. Of the dozen, I had the least direct personal involvement with the dynamics of the controversy, at least at its beginnings at the Biltmore Conference in October 1967, when BUUC was formed. At that time, as I have mentioned, I was completing a ministry to the Unitarian Church in Cape Town, South Africa. My years in South Africa had exposed me to state-sponsored racism as virulent and unabashed as that practiced in the pre–civil rights American south. It had also shown me the power of and the dangers courted by small groups of dedicated men and women who were opposed to state-sanctioned racism.

Because racism, often masked and subtle in U.S. society, was not only visible but aggressively displayed in South Africa, I had the advantage of some minimal understanding at the outset of the Empowerment Controversy. In addition, my being in South Africa during most of the 1960s had prevented my involvement in the American Civil Rights movement, thus curtailing the deep emotional attachment which many of my UU colleagues developed for the ideal of integration.

Without that emotional attachment to racial integration, my eyes were open to the revolutionary re-direction of liberal religion's social witness being demanded by black Unitarian Universalists at the Biltmore Hotel. The black UU leadership that had assembled in New York was giving the denomination the opportunity to confront assumptions about power, control, and leadership and to break out of the restrictions imposed by the white-sanctioned and approved "integrationist" agenda.

Yet, from the outset, this black UU leadership was resisted by the white UU power structure. It was resisted, demeaned, and discounted during the late '60s and into 1970, after which a significant black presence in UUism virtually disappeared. The absence of blacks from our congregations and committees was hardly noticed. A decade would pass before denominational attention would again focus on the issue of race. In 1983 the UUA Commission on Appraisal published its report on the period. In that same year I published "The Black Empowerment Controversy and the UUA," a transcript of a series of lectures sponsored by the Minns Committee. It was during this same period that UUA President Eugene Pickett established a racism audit of the denomination—the first attempt in a decade to address the question of racism within UUism.

This is not to say that Unitarian Universalism ignored all areas of social concern and involvement. During the 1970s the rights of other populations within UUism were addressed. Women, the elderly, and those who had suffered from discrimination based on sexual orientation found vigorous voice. But the denominational attention that had been directed toward black empowerment, directed by blacks, had shifted its focus to the needs of urban UU congregations, as a counter to what was perceived as the suburban captivity of liberal religion.

In 1972 the UUA Social Action Clearinghouse sponsored the first Center City Church Conference, which was held at the First Unitarian Church in Philadelphia, in the heart of that city. Although none of the organizations associated with the Empowerment Controversy were included in the conference agenda, individuals affiliated with BUUC/BAC and FULLBAC did participate. The keynote speaker was the Rev. Dr. Jack Mendelsohn, then serving as senior minister of the First Unitarian Society of Chicago and former member of BAC. Mendelsohn's theme was wholeness, and he stressed our liberal religious movement's "natural affinity for wholeness."[5] Our movement had begun, he said, by declaring that God is one, that Reality is one, and that both are interwoven with human dignity and personhood as parts of that Reality. The principle of wholeness, he said, is the bedrock of Unitarian Universalism: there is no individuality apart from community, and there is no community apart from shared power. Power resides in the very act of naming and defining, and the power to name and to define is supremely important for full personhood. True community is created by shared power.

This was the message at the heart of the Empowerment Controversy. Yet, in Mendelsohn's address during the twilight of the Controversy, the concept of wholeness sounded almost elegiac, as though the issues that had challenged us to act upon this foundational principle only a few years earlier had disappeared. Those issues—the sharing of power, the welcome of diversity—had not disappeared.

The problem with Mendelsohn's interpretation was not in the ideas of human mutuality and universality, but in their expression. "Wholeness" is an abstract concept; it does not convey the fears around human interaction that prevent its achievement, nor the joys that it can bring. Thus, the concept of wholeness is not emotionally compelling. The sentiments it seeks to express are better communicated by the ancient phrase "Beloved Community," which originated in the liturgical vocabulary of the Christian church and had been given current emphasis in the theolo-

91

gy of Martin Luther King, Jr. The meaning of Beloved Community was the real heart of the Empowerment Controversy.

King's theology provides the most searching critique of liberal religion's failure to embrace Beloved Community as anything other than a sentimental metaphor, and it helps us understand the Empowerment Controversy as a summons to act upon the promise of the Beloved Community. Our failure in this regard illuminates the fundamental liberal religious dilemma.

The central problem of Unitarian Universalism (and one that is consistently overlooked by its critics) is that the liberal conception of community is based too much on fear and too little on love. For all the rhetoric about "community" in UU circles, the term is not closely defined, and its perimeters are sketchily drawn. The religious liberal both desires and fears, needs and, at the same time, is threatened by community. No event in the past half-century has demonstrated this paradox more vividly than the Empowerment Controversy.

Any conception of community includes some threat to individual freedom and autonomy, the foundation of liberalism in all of its religious and secular forms. Even as we proclaim the benefits of community, we harbor a suspicion, inherent in liberalism and in human nature itself, of power residing in any hands but our own.

Because liberal religionists have been so wedded to the autonomy of the individual, we have failed to appreciate King's love-based conception of community, a re-formulation that attempts to renegotiate the relationship between love and fear.

A love-based conception of community does not disregard humanity's capacity for evil. It is not naïve. On the contrary, it offers a different understanding of love that embraces both humanity's capacity for evil as well as its potential for good. A love-based community, unlike a fear-based one, requires us to accept responsibility for the welfare of others, putting us into a positive relationship with them, while a fear-based community orients us only toward our own self-interest. This radical conception of love-based community is expressed in these startling dramatic words of King, echoing Gandhi: "You can do this and this and this hurtful thing to me—and I will still love you!" He was not talking about a sentimental

92

attachment, but remaining in community with his attacker—a community founded in love.

The Unitarian Universalist reaction to the Empowerment Controversy, however, reflected a fear-based concept of community, more closely aligned with Thomas Hobbes and John Locke than with John Dewey or Walter Rauschenbusch, let alone Henry Nelson Wieman or Martin Buber. For Locke, the social order was built on fear. The fear of having property stolen by those who had out in the struggle for security necessitated a social order that, above all, protected private property. For Hobbes, life in the state of nature was nasty and brutish, with the individual imperiled on every side by threats, so that power was necessary for self-preservation. The end result of such theorizing is that a just social order is held to be one that protects the acquisitions of the "fit" from the "unfit."

The liberal church's rejection of BAC's demands reflected a fear-based conception of community—fear of loss of capital (even though it had already been lost before BAC's demands); fear of democracy in action (as reflected in the UUA Board's failure to honor the decision of two General Assemblies); and fear of the future (in which black UUs outside of UUA control would lead UU efforts to achieve racial justice).

In all these ways, the Empowerment Controversy reveals that the liberal conception of community is based too much on fear and too little on love. This conception evidences a deeply pessimistic judgment about human nature at war with Unitarian Universalism's optimistic humanist rhetoric.

Much has been written describing the spiritual dimensions of Martin Luther King, Jr.'s Beloved Community. However, it is the social dimension that has particular relevance for Unitarian Universalists, who from our beginnings have affirmed that community rests upon a concept of human nature not as fundamentally evil, from which we need protection, but as fundamentally good, for which we need freedom and justice.

The war between these two conceptions of human nature is exemplified in King's famous "Letter from Birmingham Jail."

During the civil rights protest there, the white clergy of Birmingham, Alabama charged that King was responsible for what they perceived as the breakdown of law and order, resulting in the deterioration of local race relations. King responded:

> I have almost reached the regrettable conclusion that the Negro's great stumbling block in the stride toward free-dom is not the White Citizen's Council-er or the Ku Klux Klanner, but the white moderate who is more devoted to "order" than to justice; . . . who paternalisti-cally feels that he can set the timetable for another man's freedom. . . . I had hoped that the white moderate would understand that law and order exist for the purpose of establishing justice, and that when they fail to do this they become dangerously structured dams that block the flow of social progress.[6]

King exposed the mutual dependence of order and freedom, by which each needs the other and neither can stand in isolation. What is more, King understood that the primary difference between order and freedom goes back to our fundamental assessment of human nature as evil or good. If we begin with the belief that our nature is evil, then order and the means for maintaining restraint become the primary needs for estab-lishing human community. On the other hand, if our nature is funda-mentally good, freedom is the prime requirement for its development and expression.

In his response to the Birmingham clergy, King exposed their pref-erence for order over freedom (and, by implication, their negative assess-ment of human nature). The clergy contended that freedom depended upon a pre-established order. To their way of thinking, freedom without order could only mean chaos and anarchy. But, as King was quick to point out, order without freedom equals tyranny. Order and freedom depend on each other for their existence, inextricably bound in a relationship of mutual dependency.

King's point was that order, if it is to be distinguished from tyranny, must serve the ends not only of freedom but of justice. As he wrote, "A just law is a man-made code that squares with the moral law or the law of God. An unjust law is a code that is out of harmony with the moral law

. . . not rooted in eternal and natural law. Any law that uplifts human personality is just. Any law that degrades human personality is unjust."[7] Why? Because human personality is fundamentally good, and a just law is a law that supports and promotes human goodness.

King believed that the initial struggle for civil rights was necessary for the collective self-respect and dignity of a people whose subordination was maintained, in part, by laws that reinforced feelings of inadequacy and inferiority. The civil rights struggle attempted to liberate a people from shame and degradation, so that they could then glimpse the possibility of their personhood and achieve that potential through varied forms of social struggle. King's rich conception of civil rights extended beyond gaining the opportunity to "be Somebody" (as the slogan proclaimed) to include developing the capacity to serve others. Thus the individual rights gained were to be oriented toward a common good: the Beloved Community.

However, neither King nor the Civil Rights movement ever came to realize in any lasting way the aspirational vision of Beloved Community. The climax of the Civil Rights movement, the passage of the Civil Rights Act, occurred almost simultaneously with the cry of "Black Power," which King came to understand as a call to black people to amass political and economic strength to achieve legitimate goals. He viewed it as an attempt to combat the pervasive sense of nobodyness that hurt black people.

In King's sophisticated understanding, racism was much more than an irrational act of conscious prejudice and discrimination. He understood the unconscious and institutional dimensions of racism that were later unpacked by black nationalists and movingly conveyed in UU Benjamin Scott's *The Coming of the Black Man*.[8] King understood that material power relationships help constitute and reproduce a society that is unconsciously as well as consciously racist. Therefore, he invariably connected the call for integration with the demand for substantive reallocations of power. "On the one hand," he contended, "integration is true intergroup, interpersonal living. On the other hand, it is the mutual sharing of power."[9]

Today the topic of reparations has again become news. Robert Westley's article book *Many Billions Gone* suggests that a private trust be established, to be funded out of the general revenues of the United States for ten years, to accomplish the educational and economic empowerment of African Americans.[10] Randall Robinson, in his book *The Debt: What America Owes Blacks*, says, "No nation can enslave a race of people for hundreds of years, set them free bedraggled and penniless, pit them, without assistance in a hostile environment, against privileged victimizers, and then reasonably expect the gap between the heirs of the two groups to narrow. Lines, begun parallel and left alone, can never touch."[11]

King himself, in his 1963 book *Why We Can't Wait*, proposed a Bill of Rights for the Disadvantaged (whites as well as African Americans), which included a clear call for reparations for the victimization and exploitation of our ancestors, both blacks and disadvantaged whites, and as well as present-day degradations: "The moral justification for special measures," wrote King, "is rooted in the robberies inherent in the institution of slavery. It is a simple matter of justice."[12]

King's assessment of racism and its causes and cures led him to a much closer examination of the dynamics of class relations than the liberal emphasis on individual worth and merit generally permitted. Building on Walter Rauschenbusch's Social Gospel, King's Beloved Community is one in which life is interdependent and interrelated. Unlike the liberal "I" of autonomous individualism, in the Beloved Community there is no "I" without "thou." We are woven into a single garment of destiny, said King. This alternative vision captures the best of liberalism, embracing a healthy concern for self re-oriented away from an obsession with personal blame, guilt, and causation. It redirects the self toward service to God and humanity that symbolizes the interdependency and sacredness of life. When self-love is linked to other-love that is linked, in turn, to divine spiritual love, both humility and possibility are nurtured. We understand, finally, the social, spiritual, and strategic dimensions of holistic community.

King's concept of the Beloved Community does not rest solely upon Euro-American philosophy and religion. The voice of Africa is also present here in the concept of *ubuntu*, a metaphor for human interdependence. *Ubuntu*, best translated as "a person is a person through persons," is at the heart of traditional African society. It is rooted in the African sense of divine presence as being primarily within people; it is in relation to other people that the African person attains her or his full humanity.

Over time, *ubuntu* has evolved into a metaphor for interdependence. According to D. A. Masolo, *ubuntu* means "humanity," the category of intelligent human force that includes spirit, the human dead, the living, and the *ubuntu* which is God's being.[13]

The former South African archbishop Desmond Tutu is probably the best-known exponent, and indeed an embodiment, of *ubuntu*. Tutu has written that "a person is not basically an independent solitary entity. A person is human precisely in being enveloped in the community of other human beings, in being caught up in the bundle of life."[14]

Ubuntu theology, no less than the social gospel of Rauschenbusch, the humanism of Wieman, the Jewish mysticism of Buber, and the beloved community of King, offers an alternative to the central problem undermining the liberal religious approach to racism: liberalism's commitment to an abstract individualism that refuses to see the individual as constructed by race and other group identities that shape perspectives.

Liberalism in general, and Unitarian Universalism in particular, is preoccupied with individual mind-set and individual consciousness. Its understanding of the individual as an autonomous being who can pick, choose, and sit in judgment while disconnected from culture, history, and community is the source of the problem. Such institutional change as did occur during the Empowerment Controversy came at the expense of finger-pointing and blaming someone else's "racism" as the cause of the problem, rather than examining the situation in total. This created unnecessary psychological resistance to needed change.

A holistic *ubuntu*-inspired social awareness could have made the difference. In the love-based, *ubuntu*-inspired conception of community, life is envisioned as interrelated and interdependent. Recall again the work of Henry Hampton, the producer of the television masterpiece *Eyes on the Prize*. When asked in 1984 about his commitment to preserving the historical record of the struggles of blacks and working Americans, Hampton grew philosophical. Acknowledging that Americans seemed impatient with history, preferring to envision the future rather than explore the past, he sided with the ancient Greeks, who saw the lessons of history as the only thing protecting the present from being swallowed by the tidal wave of the future, which invariably crashes upon it with devastating force.

Hampton's death in 1997 struck both the media and liberal communities with tidal force. Those who had known him assembled at Boston's historic Arlington Street Church in witness to his legacy as a professional filmmaker and civil rights activist whose commitments to justice and truth were profound and unshakable.

As a Unitarian Universalist, Hampton had gone to Selma, Alabama in 1965 in support of King's civil rights struggle. Two years later he had joined the black caucus that assembled in a hotel room during the UU Department of Social Responsibility's meeting to formulate a response to the "black rebellion." He had been a vigorous supporter of the formation of BUUC and a major voice in initial attempts to explain its goals to UUs.

While Hampton's career as a filmmaker introduced him to millions, his work as a committed African American Unitarian Universalist remains a touchstone for UUs seeking to understand the transitions the denomination experienced during the late 1960s and early 1970s.

Sitting in the Arlington Street Church during the memorial service, listening to the words of eulogy, I felt that Hampton's life, and especially his life as a Unitarian Universalist, reflected a commitment to Beloved Community as sincere and passionate as that of Martin Luther King, Jr. himself. And those gathered together in that sanctuary, African American and Euro-American together, secure in their own power, were united in their common love. This was Unitarian Universalism in its fullness and its strength of purpose, an epiphany of the Beloved Community.

In recent years Unitarian Universalists have heard calls for greater racial diversity in our association. To that end, organizations such as Diverse Revolutionary Unitarian Universalist Multicultural Ministries (DRUUM) have been created. We have also elected an African American as UUA president. While such initiatives are worthy and welcome, the fact of increased racial diversity in our pews, pulpits, presidential offices will not, by itself, achieve the goal of Beloved Community. In her magisterial study of the growing religious diversity in this country, Diana Eck, a professor of comparative religion and Indian studies at the Harvard Divinity

School, has pointed out that the United States is fast becoming the most religiously diverse nation on earth, but that diversity does not necessarily translate into community. Eck's distinction between diversity and pluralism is essential for us. According to Eck, "Religious diversity is an observable fact of American life today, but diversity is not pluralism, which requires engagement, active participation and attunement to the life and the energies of one another."[15]

Our Unitarian Universalist endorsement of diversity, and our need of it in our congregations, suggests that we must update and revise our time-tested principle of tolerance, which has too often functioned as a means to avoid grappling with the thorny issues that result from deep engagement. Whereas tolerance can create a climate of restraint and respect, at least on a superficial level, it does not necessarily move us to attune ourselves to the life and the energies of another, especially when that carries the threat of exposure to past and present wrongs and hurts.

A 1908 article by the Rev. John Haynes Holmes, entitled "Unitarianism and the Social Question," expresses the hope that the denomination would find a way to "seek the causes of social diseases and their eradication." But, writes Holmes, "it must be admitted that our exaggerated notions of freedom, our tradition of individualism and our inherited conservatism as a people of the upper classes all seem against it."[16]

The three impediments listed by Holmes remain with us, and in fact they have increased since his time. They are the three "locked doors" that keep us confined to the "discovered country" of well-worn liberal religious traditions and attitudes.

Perhaps by the very act of recognizing the limits of our traditional vision we can move beyond fear, denial, and guilt toward a renewed commitment to mutuality, interdependence, and coalition-building that risks engagement with difference—the three modalities that have the power to expand our vision, liberate our sense of justice, and move us from where we are toward where we ought to go.

Notes

1. Donald McKinney, verbal response to lecture on Empowerment Controversy, February 21, 2002.
2. Lisa Ward, "The Black Empowerment Controversy within the UUA, 1967–1970," M.Div. thesis, Union Theological Seminary, 1991.
3. McKinney, response to lecture, February 21, 2002.
4. Alicia McNary Forsey, ed., *In Their Own Words: A Conversation with Participants in the Black Empowerment Movement within the Unitarian Universalist Association* (Berkeley, CA: Starr King School for the Ministry, 2001).
5. Jack Mendelsohn, "The City: Being in It and Being of It," address delivered at the Center City Church Conference, Philadelphia, October 1971.
6. Martin Luther King, Jr., "Letter from Birmingham Jail," *A Testimony of Hope* (San Francisco: Harper and Row, 1964), p. 295.
7. *Ibid.*
8. Benjamin Scott, *The Coming of the Black Man* (Boston: Beacon Press, 1968).
9. *Ibid.*
10. Robert Westley, "Many Billions Gone," *Boston College Law Review*, June 1999.
11. Randall Robinson, *The Debt: What America Owes Blacks* (New York: Plume/Penguin, 2000), p. 74.
12. Martin Luther King, Jr., *Why We Can't Wait* (New York: New American Library, 1964).
13. D. A. Masolo, *African Philosophy in Search of Identity* (Bloomington, IN: Indiana University Press, 1994), p. 87.
14. Desmond Tutu, "Viability," in *Recent Theology for Africa* (Durban: Lutheran Publishing House, 2001), p. 38.
15. Diana Eck, *A New Religious America* (New York: Harper Collins, 2001), p. 70.
16. John Haynes Holmes, "Unitarianism and the Social Question," *The Unitarian*, 1908; quoted in Ward, "The Black Empowerment Controversy," p. 19.